WALK

WITH

CHRIST

David Haas

ORIGINAL ART BY
JAN RICHARDSON

CELEBRATING THE WAY OF THE NATIVITY, THE CROSS, AND THE RESURRECTION

Published by Clear Faith Publishing, LLC
22 Lafayette Road
Princeton, NJ 08540

ISBN 978-1-940414-07-2

Cover and Interior Design by Doug Cordes
Author photo by Helen Haas

WALK

WITH

CHRIST

David Haas

ORIGINAL ART BY
JAN RICHARDSON

CELEBRATING THE WAY OF THE NATIVITY, THE CROSS, AND THE RESURRECTION

FOR MY

GOOD FRIEND AND TEACHER,

Arthur E. Zannoni,

MY "BIBLE-HERO," WHOSE

PASSION FOR THE WORD

ENLIGHTENS ME TO

"COME, SEE, AND FOLLOW"

MORE DEEPLY.

TABLE OF CONTENTS

GRATITUDE

I want to offer my deepest thanks to Jim Knipper of Clear Faith Publishing, and to my friends, guides, teachers and mentors in the pathways of scripture and preaching over the years: Fr. Bill Taylor, Art Zannoni, Fr. Michael Joncas, Megan McKenna, Fr. Ray East, Sr. Kathleen Harmon, SNDdeN, Fr. Ray Kemp, Bill Huebsch, Rev. Walter Brueggeman, Fr. Michael Byron, Marva Dawn, Fr. Michael Crosby, Capuchin; James Moudry, Fr. Joe Kempf, Rory Cooney, Fr. Richard Rohr, OFM; John Dominic Crossan, Fr. George DeCosta, Sr. Diane Bergant, CSA; Bishop John Shelby Spong, Fr. Ed Foley, Capuchin; Sr. Barbara Reid, OP; Bishop Remi De Roo, Pearl Gervais, Fr. James Bessert, Fr. Bob DeLand, Fr. Paul Jaroszeski, Fr. John Forliti, Rev. Anita Bradshaw, Fr. Roc O'Connor, SJ; and Fr. Robert Duggan.

I also want to give thanks to God for those heroes who have gone before us, who "broke open" the Word not only through their tremendous scholarship, but also by the very witness of their lives: Fr. Eugene LaVerdiere, SSS; Marcus Borg, Fr. Raymond Brown, SS; Fr. Henri Nouwen, Bishop Kenneth Untener, Sr. Roberta Kolasa, SJ; Fr. Jeffrey Donner, Fr. James Dunning, and Fr. Walter Burghardt, SJ.

I especially want to give thanks to Jan Richardson for her tremendous art and the windows into the spiritual journey that her gift brings not only to this book of stations, but to all seekers who encounter her visual story. It is a true honor that her work is serving as a visual partner for the journey.

Finally, I would like to express my love-filled thanks to Sr. Kathleen Storms, SSND; Bonnie Faber, Stephen Pishner and Lori True for their unfailing friendships and support, and to Helen for always believing in my many creative pursuits.

FOREWORD

David Haas knows how to compose and direct liturgical music. Along with Michael Joncas and Marty Haugen, David makes up a trinity of the most sung contemporary settings of music for the sacraments in North America. My guess is that they are so familiar to getting us through the liveliest, and redeeming the duller Sunday gatherings of Christians, that we take them for granted unless we are in the business of picking and practicing selections.

But David Haas and true Church musicians are ministers in schools and parishes, as well as artists. Ministers are listeners before they "do" anything. Listening to one's heart and to those who make up our communities rarely gets a mention in any job description or strategic parish plan. It is the crucial activity for those who would touch a heart: take in the one or the ones before you in all their glory and complexity. The embrace is more than a hug or a gesture. Inviting people into their depth and your own is the deepest virtue.

Walk With Christ, the beautiful book you have before you, is a series of prompts for just a closer walk, a deeper form of cardio exercise. And it comes from the hand of one who has listened deeply from the Emmaus Center; with the students at Cretin-Derham Hall High School and the summer *Music Ministry Alive!* program, and at St. Cecilia's Parish, all in and around St. Paul. David Haas has spent quality time with folks all over God's world, assisting them to get to their story before ever coming to share that story with others. If that reminds you of one of my favorites, google "Song of the Body of Christ."

The stational format of these prompts using the whole of the life and ministry of Jesus and the church of the Acts of the Apostles, is genius and genuine. Few of us see our stages of life or our day to day as 'stations' in our pilgrimage. Stop and refresh. Then, onward we go to another station.

Very few of our buttoned-down churches do processionals in the streets like many another cultures. Pity! We may watch marches or sing while those who minister at the altar enter the space. Some few have taken the Stations of the Cross into the streets. And our wonderful Latino Majority keeps us alive, both to the passion and to the glories of Our Lady of Guadalupe, stopping traffic a couple of times a year and raising prayer and song through city avenues.

Here, in this handy format of moments in the life of our Christ, David Haas lifts us from the sedentary to an active, moving reflection as we walk with Jesus. This is not a lonesome highway. We can partner one another through the Word, the prayer, the quiet and the song that may stir.

A recent session with Terry, who was troubled in his blended family situation, led to a question of how he spends his day. We use questions to find the time that already has been made for stillness. Terry takes a walk every day after work. Half an hour. I suggested he walk with Jesus and a favorite scripture, and showed him a few from the daily lectionary. The idea was communicated but the feeling was awkward. After another half hour or so he left. I knew he could handle my suggestion, but I felt like I had blown him off with "The Daily Word" or some such generic remedy.

The next reading I did was this manuscript. "Geez, this is a zinger. David is grabbing me." David knows about life and love, relationships and brokenness, dreams and dreams deferred. After a few takes over some days, Jesus was communicating. David was wherever he was. I was with Jesus. I am going to give Terry and myself of this companion. Food for the walk.

Good friends are making the *Camino de Santiago* across Spain to Compostela as I write. Emilio Estevez' *The Way* with Martin Sheen captures some aspects of that pilgrimage to the Saint of Compostela. Receiving daily posts from second and third-timers doing the *Camino* brings home her personal journey of reflection and meditations as they climb and descend. Much of what is being shared is picked up in David's telling. Life is so much more than the Cross, but its shadow is never too far from the Joyful, the Glorious and the Luminous sides of life. There is a time for everything under heaven. And Haas knows how to keep time.

Use this book. This is more morning food for me heading into the day and the workout or walk. It may suit you at some other time. Terry may use it at the end of his work day before his walk. The Scripture and the cues have a staying power. The WALK WITH CHRIST enlivens me. WALK ON!

Rev. Raymond Kemp
Georgetown University
Washington, DC

HOW TO PRAY AND WALK
WITH THE "WAY"

These paths of prayer call out to be more than just an opportunity to "look back" and remember a historical story; it is an opportunity to discover a "way" for us all to embrace more deeply, right here, right now. This type of "station-centered" prayer is a call to conversion, hopefully moving forward toward a more disciplined transformation throughout the entirety of our lives. In fact, it is more than just one "way." The Gospels provide a contrasting set of "ways" through the unique eyeglasses of the four evangelists, Matthew, Mark, Luke and John. While they provide an obvious approach to prayer individually and with others during the liturgical seasons of Advent-Christmas, Lent and Easter, these patterns can become an ongoing practice throughout any time of the liturgical year.

Walk With Christ is intended to help promote a keeping of this prayerful path, centered in the "Word" and meditating on the "Walk" in our lives as contemporary believers and followers. May they truly enlighten our faith as we come to know and celebrate the Christ that is presented to us in the Gospels, as truly the way, truth, and life.

David Haas

BORN

WITH

CHRIST

**THE WAY OF THE NATIVITY
WITH MATTHEW AND LUKE**

Through the winter and the cold,
our faith can weaken and grow old;
so we ache to find a song
of a God, one to whom we can belong.
Instead of power shown as might,
a tiny baby is your light;
we find a child who sings the way,
come now, be born in us today.

Christmas comes and Christmas goes,
yet pain and violence sadly grow.
We cry and hurt, when will it end?
Is there a Savior, a Messiah whom you'll send?
We pray in hope, please hear our cry,
or is the story just a lie?
We need the child to show the way,
come now, be born in us today.

In this time of joy and cheer,
we find resentment, bound by fear;
called to believe, but we are blind,
give us a reason, a life-line we can find.
Poisoned by selfishness and hate,
how much longer must we wait?
This child brings life to our decay,
come now, be born in us today.

Give us a sign that you are real,
numb though we are, help us to feel.
There's only one gift that we need,
A manger, too, where all can come and feed.
We need to know we're not alone,
a place of safety, a home.
Although the cross is here to stay,
come now, be born in us today.[1]

While Advent is most certainly not a "mini-Lent," and Christmas is not the central story of what it means to live in Christ—the Incarnation cycle is prologue and also a continual ongoing story that needs to be celebrated, especially beyond the often manipulated and over-sugary versions that we annually hear and endure.

So this "way" of the birth of Jesus is offered here as a way of keeping this season of Advent-Christmas, not as two separate seasons, but a single mystery that we can and should linger over in our life of prayer. The Gospels of Matthew and Luke provide for us a path, a template that we can follow, observe, and pray, not just for our own personal spiritual life, but also as a call to discipleship. This season, which is intended to be a time of joy and celebration, is for many a time of sadness, loneliness, and even despair. Lent is not the only season in which we confront the Paschal Mystery. Rather, it finds a beginning in the mystery of the Nativity. This Jesus comes to us, not in a grand and triumphal procession, but in the simplicity of a child born into a family and race on the margins, with all of the hope and possibility that each newborn can bring.

It is my hope and prayer that praying these Stations of the Nativity, we can find Christmas again for the first time, and discover that presence in our hearts and in those in most need of hearing "tidings of great joy."

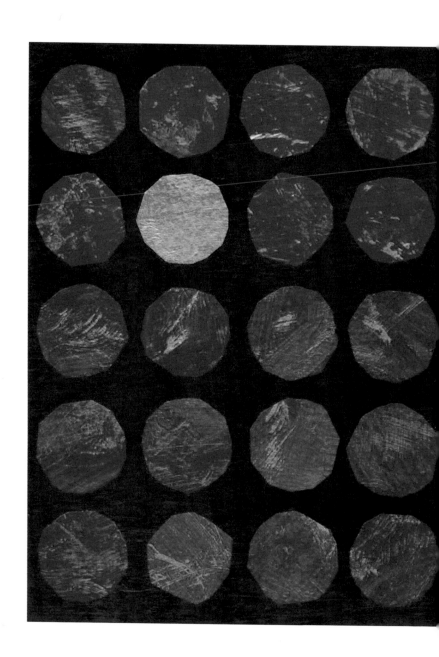

Where Advent Begins

THE FIRST STATION

Zechariah

In the days of King Herod of Judea,
there was a priest named Zechariah.
Once when he was serving as priest before God,
then there appeared to him an angel of the Lord,
standing at the right side of the altar of incense.

When Zechariah saw him,
he was terrified; and fear overwhelmed him.
But the angel said to him,
"Do not be afraid, Zechariah,
for your prayer has been heard.
Your wife will bear you a son,
and you will name him John.
You will have joy and gladness,
and many will rejoice at his birth,
for he will be great in the sight of the Lord."

Zechariah said to the angel,
"How will I know that this is so?

For I am an old man,
and my wife is getting on in years."
The angel replied,
"I am Gabriel.
I stand in the presence of God,
And I have been sent to speak to you
and to bring you this good news.
But now,
because you did not believe my words,
which will be fulfilled in their time,
you will become mute, unable to speak,
until the day these things occur."

Luke 1:5a; 8a; 11-15; 18-20

THE WALK

Sometimes, when we hear amazingly good news, it can be far too much for us to believe, contain, and take in. It is very easy to become cynical or to have very low expectations, and so it becomes very difficult to believe in glory and joy when gloom and apathy so often rue the day. So we are slow to believe. We are hesitant to invest our hearts in news and promises that seem to so often, result in disappointment and dashed hopes. But God is patient with us, and God's love remains consistent and unending. For us, the time of waiting can be exasperating. But the patience and steadiness of God is almost maddening because God refuses to give up on us. Our time of waiting is restless. God's time of waiting is purposeful, even creative, always colored and trimmed with love, and endlessly true to the promises given. Our doubts can grab us by the throat. God's compassion is always lavish, gentle, filled with covenants never to be broken.

We lose hope all too readily. God's ache for our knowing and experiencing fulfillment is eternal. Our being manically realistic blinds us. God enlightens us with amazing things, over and over again.

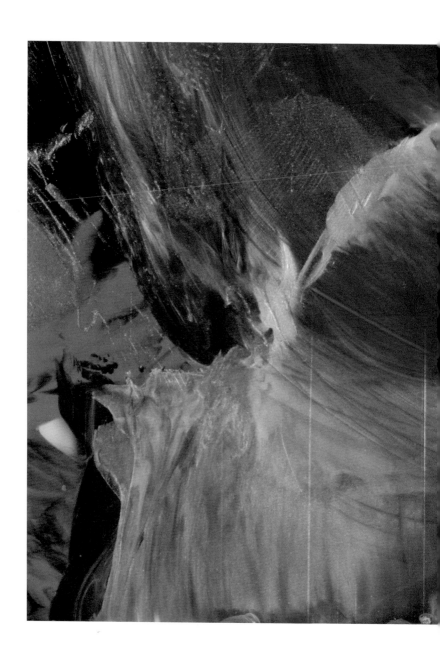

Gabriel and Mary

THE SECOND STATION

The Annunciation

In the sixth month
the angel Gabriel was sent by God
to a town in Galilee called Nazareth,
to a virgin engaged to a man whose name was Joseph,
of the house of David.
The virgin's name was Mary.
And he came to her and said,
"Greetings, favored one! The Lord is with you.
But she was much perplexed by his words
and pondered what sort of greeting
this might be.
The angel said to her,
"Do not be afraid, Mary,
for you have found favor with God.
And now, you will conceive in your womb
and bear a son,
and you will name him Jesus.
He will be great,

and will be called the Son of the Most High,
and the Lord God will give to him.
He will reign over the house of Jacob forever,
and of his kingdom there will be no end."
Mary said to angel,
"How can this be, since I am a virgin?"
The angel said to her,
"The Holy Spirit will come upon you,
and the power of the Most High will overshadow you;
therefore, the child to be born will be holy;
he will be called Son of God.
And now, your relative Elizabeth in her old age
has also conceived a son;
and this is the sixth month for her
who was said to be barren.
For nothing will be impossible with God."
Then Mary said,
"Here am I, the servant of the Lord;
let it be with me according to your word."

Luke 1:26-38a

THE WALK

To truly accept and do the will of God is very, very hard
indeed. Most of the time, we never intentionally pray
for it, as we can be frightened by what God will ask of
us. To take the leap of faith with a yes that is unequiv-
ocal, filled with investment and confidence, seems rare
and usually impossible. There are too many cautions,
too many "what ifs," too much strategic and critical
thinking needed, filled with so many potential circumstances to consider. Mary is filled with the Holy Spirit,
and there is only one response possible for her: "Here
am I, the servant of the Lord." And this highly unlikely

young teenager, who is both nobody and, at the same time, everybody, gives her assent with delight. The Word was strong for her and, although poor, she offers her sacrifice in order to welcome and nurture the child with the most profound humility. She gives her yes, accepting his destiny as teacher, healer, prophet and vessel of mercy, and also, his ultimate execution and destruction because of his being and witnessing the very Incarnation of God. The call here seems too risky and fraught with danger, imbued with the real possibility of failure. But nothing is impossible with God.

Magnificat

THE THIRD STATION

The Visitation

THE WORD

In those days Mary set out and went with haste
to a Judean town in the hill country,
where she entered the house of Zechariah and
greeted Elizabeth.
When Elizabeth heard Mary's greeting,
the child leaped in her womb.
And Elizabeth was filled with Holy Spirit
and exclaimed with a loud cry,
"Blessed are you among women,
and blessed is the fruit of your womb,
And why has this happened to me,
that the mother of my Lord comes to me?
For as soon as I heard the sound of your greeting,
the child in my womb leaped for joy.
And blessed is she who believed that there would be
a fulfillment of what was spoken to her by the Lord."

And Mary said,
"My soul magnifies the Lord,
and my spirit rejoices in God my Savior,
for he has looked with favor
on the lowliness of his servant.
Surely, from now on all generations will call be blessed;
for the Mighty One has done great things for me,
and holy is his name.
His mercy is for those who fear him
from generation to generation.
He has shown the strength with his arm;
he has scattered the proud in the thoughts of their hearts.
He has brought down the powerful from their thrones,
and lifted up the lowly;
he has filled the hungry with good things,
and sent the rich away empty.
He has helped his servant Israel,
in remembrance of his mercy,
according to the promise he made to our ancestors,
to Abraham and to his descendants forever."

Luke 1:39-55

THE WALK

In some nations throughout the world, this prayer of the *Magnificat* is not translated from Latin into the local language because the text stirs up trouble, economically and politically. This song of Mary tells us much about God, about a different approach to celebrating Christmas, and God's vision of what it means to follow and become a disciple. Mary is young, vulnerable, poor and marginalized, and yet she becomes the vehicle for God's redemptive vision. This is because far too many in our world are vulnerable and marginalized. Bottom line – God cares for *all* people and is deeply concerned about how human life is realized. God aches and cries for people who are hungry, homeless, oppressed, and wracked with suffering and pain. This song, this canticle, should make us very uncomfortable, and we should squirm uneasily every time we hear or pray it. Because the reality is that far too many children are abused and neglected. Far too many people are homeless and alone. Far too many people are victims of injustice and hatred. Far too many people are shunned and reaching out for compassion. Far too many people live in conditions caused by our economy and tax structure, deepening the canyons between the rich and the poor. God does not want to scold us, but is passionately attempting to break through and show us that the child born into our midst is not coming to be cute, but to reveal to us a different way of living, through the embrace of God.

Benedictus

THE FOURTH STATION

The Birth of the Baptist

THE WORD

Now the time came for Elizabeth to give birth,
and she bore a son.
Her neighbors and relatives heard that the Lord
had shown his great mercy to her,
and they rejoiced with her.

On the eighth day they came to circumcise the child,
and they were going to name him Zechariah after
his father.
But his mother said,
"No, he is to be called John."
Then they began motioning to his father
to find out what name he wanted to give him.
He asked for a writing tablet and wrote,
"His name is John."
And all of them were amazed.
Immediately his mouth was opened and his
tongue freed,

and he began to speak, praising God.
Fear came over all their neighbors,
and all these things were talked about
throughout the entire hill country of Judea.
All who heard them pondered them and said,
"What then will this child become?"
For indeed, the hand of the Lord was with him.

Then his father Zechariah was filled with the
Holy Spirit
and spoke this prophecy:
"Blessed be the Lord God of Israel,
for he has looked favorably on this people and
redeemed them.
He has raised up a mighty Savior for us
in the house of his servant David,
as he spoke through the mouths of his holy prophets
of old,
that we would be saved from our enemies
and from the hand of all who hate us.
Thus he has shown mercy promised to our ancestors,
and has remembered his holy Covenant,
the oath that he swore to our ancestor Abraham,
to grant us that we,
being rescued from the hands of our enemies,
might serve him without fear, in holiness and
righteousness
before him all our days.
And you, child, will be called the prophet of the
Most High;
For you will go before the Lord
to prepare his ways,
to give knowledge of salvation to his people
by the forgiveness of their sins.
By the tender mercy of our God,
the dawn from on high will break upon us,
to give light to those who sit in darkness

and in the shadow of death,
to guide our feet into the way of peace."

Luke 1:57-79

THE WALK

We have reason to hope, but not in the Gospel of prosperity and success that seems to suggest that God wants us all to be well and prosperous. Rather, it is the message and music of forgiveness that this presence of God will bring about. The birth of the Baptist brings to the forefront all that John was doing constantly in his ministry of water and mercy. He is always pointing beyond himself. His finger-pointing is trying to steer our attention toward how God is with us, and how we are to be toward God, prophesied in Zechariah's song of "the tender mercy of our God," singing of a time and place where God will "guide our feet into the way of peace." The mercy, oath, and promise that God grants us can be a source of our healing and salvation. This time, this place is one of wholeness and contentment. This time, this place is one where redemption is not something that we are "guilted" into believing, but a gift that can transform injustice and chaos into a blessing of God's love, peacemaking, and love lavishly shared. And this place is for all, especially for the poor and the powerless.

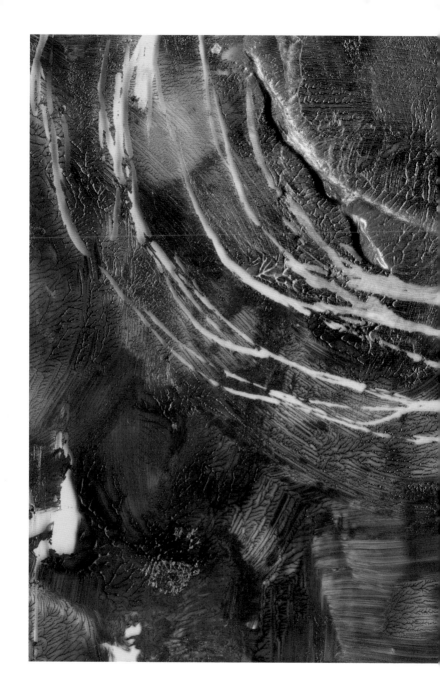

Christ in My Dreaming

THE FIFTH STATION

Joseph's Dream

Now the birth of Jesus the Messiah took place
in this way.
When his mother Mary had been engaged to Joseph,
but before they lived together,
she was found to be with child from the Holy Spirit.
Her husband Joseph,
being a righteous man and unwilling to expose her
to public disgrace,
planned to dismiss her quietly.
But just when he had resolved to do this,
and angel of the Lord appeared to him in a dream
and said,
"Joseph, son of David,
do not be afraid to take Mary as your wife,
for the child conceived in her is from the Holy Spirit.
She will bear a son,
and you are to name him Jesus,
for he will save his people from their sins.
All of this took place through the prophet:
"Look, the virgin shall conceive and bear a son,

and they shall name him Emmanuel,
which means, "God is with us."
When Joseph awoke from sleep,
he did as the angel of the Lord commanded him.

Matthew 1:18-24a

THE WALK

We have heard this reading many times. Many of us may actually have it committed to memory. These are deep words that fill the heart. But we need to be careful of the nostalgia that often has a stranglehold on the meaning of Christmas, with the many pageants, plays, and over-romanticized stagings of the birth of Jesus. They have the potential to allow us to slip into a creche' "coma," in which we reduce this redemptive story to sheep, donkeys, shepherds, wise men, angels and Mary and Joseph gazing into the crib, complete with a star overhead. Sometimes even Santa shows up at these re-enactments. Often the logistics and performances of the pageant do not go perfectly, but that is exactly the point. Our children actually "get it" more completely. Birthing is not an exact science, and like it is for us, the birth of Jesus was messy, unprepared, filled with chaos and challenging circumstances. Add to that, the noise and smell, and the unpleasant conditions of a stable. This mother was a teenager accompanied by a man much older than her, who most certainly underwent cruelty and judgment by a people who probably saw her beginning to show, knowing full well that she was not yet married. Joseph is one who must be embarrassed, knowing that he is not the father, but at the same time, a good man who refuses to punish and shame; who operates and makes decisions by unlikely sources: angel appearances and dreams. We know that the name Emmanuel means "God with us," and this presence is given light in people who are at the margins: the poor, homeless and vulnerable. God knows what it is to be pushed to the outside, and is passionate about compassion and justice in this world. These are deep words that are very important, hopeful and yes, radical. Because these words come and live in dreams, dreams that bring the light into the world.

A Home for God

THE SIXTH STATION

The Birth of Jesus

THE WORD

In those days a decree went out from Emperor Augustus
that all the world should be registered.
All went to their own towns to be registered.
Joseph also went from the town of Nazareth in Galilee
to Judea,
to the city of David called Bethlehem,
because he was descended from the house and
family of David.
He went to be registered with Mary,
to whom he was engaged and who was expecting
a child.
When they were there,
The time came for her to deliver her child.

And she gave birth to her firstborn son
and wrapped him in bands of cloth,
and laid him in a manger,
because there was no place for them in the inn.

Luke 2:1, 3-7

THE WALK

Those of us, who may believe that faith and politics should not be mixed together, need to consider this story. We hear it every year at Midnight Mass (whenever it is scheduled), and it is a story that is highly political, asking us to reject established notions of empire and power, to intentionally live in contradiction to the societal way of doing things. Mary and Joseph are forced to undertake a perilous journey to Bethlehem from Nazareth, and they are *us*, in so many ways. They are refugees trying to navigate a path through chaos along with others on similar journeys. In the midst of the disruptive chaos of our world, new birth is happening all around us, if we pay attention. Jesus was born a child of a poor and conquered country. Like Jesus, many of our poor are often seen as expendable. For the poor, there is "no place for them," and are often pushed to the outer boundaries of life, attempting to find new birth in the midst of what seems to be a hungry and dying world. The manger, the "feeding trough," is in a way a "tabernacle" that houses the Bread of Life proclaiming a feast of justice and liberation. Mangers were made of stone, and because this is so, it foreshadows the empty "stone tomb" into which the dead body of Jesus is placed. We are born, and we also die. *How* we are born, with *whom* we are born, and *for whom* we are born is important. It was for Christ. It needs to be the same with us.

THE SEVENTH STATION

The Shepherds and Angels

THE WORD

In that region there were shepherds living in the fields,
keeping watch over the flock by night.
Then an angel of the Lord stood before them,
and the glory of the Lord shone around them,
and they were terrified.
But the angel said to them,
"Do not be afraid; for see –
I am bringing you good news of great joy
for all the people:
to you is born this day in the city of David a Savior,
who is the Messiah, the Lord.
This will be a sign for you:
you will find a child wrapped in bands of cloth
and lying in a manger.
And suddenly, there with the angels was
a multitude of the heavenly host,
praising God and saying,
"Glory to God in the highest heaven,
and on earth peace among those whom he favors!"

Luke 2: 8-14

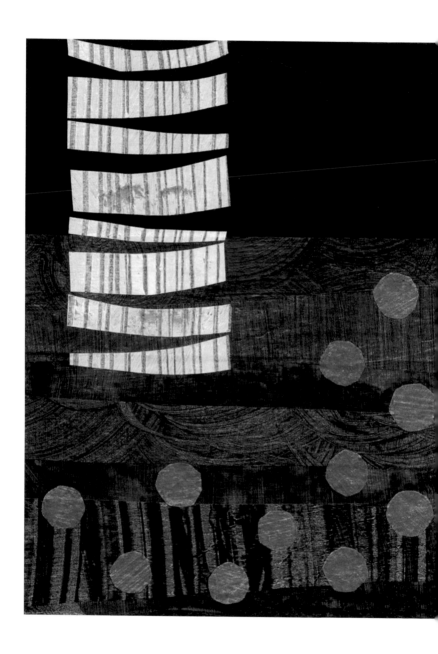

Glory

THE WALK

The Incarnation of "God with us" brings in a new world order; where God intentionally dwells and identifies with all who live a life of humiliation, poverty and injustice. Here, we find that it is shepherds, the poor and dregs of society, who receive the first announcement of this birth. This is a blast of a trumpet bearing "good news of great joy" for those whom good news has only perhaps been a naïve dream. Often believed to be lazy and incompetent, and believed to be actual criminals, they were often treated with distain. It is these shepherds, these "criminals" who are the ones whose ears are awakened by the song of the angels. We have so many similar shepherds today, those who come from different cultures or sexual orientation; many are the homeless and the physically and mentally challenged. Angels are announcing a new reign, a new light to follow. To who, and with whom, do we share this "good news?" We are talking about the birth of more than a child, but more profoundly, a birth of a new Kingdom, a new realm of God's vision.

Treasured in Her Heart

THE EIGHTH STATION

The Shepherds at the Manger

THE WORD

When the angels had left them and gone into heaven,
the shepherds said to one another,
"Let us go now to Bethlehem and see this thing
that has taken place,
which the Lord has made known to us."
So they went with haste and found Mary and Joseph,
and the child lying in the manger.
When they saw this,
they made known what had been told them about
this child;
and all who heard it were amazed
at what the shepherds told them.
But Mary treasured all these words
and pondered them in her heart.
The shepherds returned,
glorifying and praising God for all that they had
heard and seen,
as it had been told them.

Luke 2:15-20

THE WALK

Being a shepherd requires being attentive to one's flock, and overseeing their grazing and growth, assuring their protection. For these shepherds, this meant that they were unable to leave and take part with the ritual community, leading to discrimination and disdain from religious leaders. But they leave their economic security to answer a call. They abandon the established sense of safety to embrace a new vision. In faith we are summoned to leave behind all that we believe keeps us safe, practical and sensible. In faith, we are charged to seek out God's presence, and to do so in the most unlikely or "un-religious" places. Sometimes we will be led, and other times, we must intentionally seek out the mangers that hold the most precious of gifts, the most treasured of signs that can lead us all to see and understand. We make haste like shepherds, embarking on a journey to see God's glory in the simple, ordinary, yet profound presence of a child. Born for us. We do not have to travel back in history to know and be blessed by this presence. It is found in the new births that occur every day in our lives. Not just with the wonderful and beautiful babies that are born. But also in any human heart that is born anew. Like the shepherds who were awakened to this presence, may we all make haste to discover and share it as well.

THE NINTH STATION

The Naming of Jesus

THE WORD

After eight days had passed,
it was time to circumcise the child;
and he was called Jesus,
the name given by the angel
before he was conceived in the womb.

Luke 2:21

THE WALK

The names that we choose for our children are important. The numerous choices are, of course, infinite. But this decision is still important. Because this is how we will look at and refer to this human being throughout their lives. It contains and holds a sense of self for those receiving such a name. The name "Jesus" is a form of the name "Joshua," a most popular name in ancient

Baptized and Beloved

times. It means "the Lord delivers." Jesus is interpreted through his name, which is also his life purpose: God will deliver through him. When we hear the words that his name is "the name that is above every other name" (Philippians 2:9), we submit our own names as real, true, and standing with Jesus. His name, and our name, is a signal that makes us real to another. By our own name and identity, we help to "deliver" each other from harm. We too, through the power of our name, following the name of Jesus, can become instruments of a new and lasting redemption. At our Baptism, we are called by name and claimed for Christ. So let us live by our name, holding the name and presence of Jesus close to our hearts.

Magi and Mystery

THE TENTH STATION

The Magi

In the time of King Herod,
after Jesus was born in Bethlehem of Judea,
wise men from the East came to Jerusalem, asking,
"Where is the child
who has been born king of the Jews?
For we observed his star at its rising,
and have come to pay him homage."
When King Herod heard this,
he was frightened,
and all Jerusalem with him;
and calling together all of the chief priests
and scribes of the people,
he inquired of them where the Messiah was to be born.
They told him,
"In Bethlehem of Judea;
for so it has been written by the prophet:
'And you, Bethlehem, in the land of Judah,
are by no means least among the rulers of Judah;

for from you shall come a ruler
who is to shepherd my people Israel.'"

Then Herod secretly called for the wise men
and learned from them
the exact time when the star had appeared.
Then he sent them to Bethlehem, saying,
"Go and search diligently for the child;
and when you have found him,
bring me word so that I may also go
and pay him homage."
When they had heard the king, they set out;
And there, ahead of them,
went the star that they had seen at its rising,
until it stopped over the place where the child was.
When they saw that the star had stopped,
they were overwhelmed with joy.
On entering the house,
they saw the child with Mary, his mother;
and they knelt down and paid him homage.
Then, opening their treasure chests,
they offered him gifts of gold, frankincense, and myrrh.

Matthew 2:1-11

THE WALK

Jesus brought, and continues to bring, light and life into
our world. The difficulty with any bearer of light is that
they scare the bejesus out of those—and to whom we far
too often give permission to—who hold power. Herod,
and many "Herod's" that flood positions of leadership in
our world, often rule and influence through the threat
of punishment and destruction. Not Jesus, and the wise
ones from the East are seeking to catch a glimpse of his

wisdom. They follow a star, a light that radiates the sky and brightens their hopes. They rely on the guidance of the Christ to lead them out of trouble and into care and protection. Jesus offers the world such guidance and protection, and his radiance offers the mercy and grace of God, lifting us all from the burdens and the terror of life. Gloom can drift away. Wounds can be healed. Shame and guilt can be replaced with forgiveness. Life can and will be lifted from our experience of loss and grief. A star, a light has come for us to follow, and we offer our greatest homage by offering the gifts of our lives for one another.

So That You May Know the Hope

THE ELEVENTH STATION

Simeon and Anna

When the time came for their purification
according to the law of Moses,
they brought him up to Jerusalem to present him.

Now there was a man in Jerusalem
whose name was Simeon.
This man was righteous and devout,
looking forward to the consolation of Israel,
and the Holy Spirit rested on him.
It had been revealed to him by the Holy Spirit
that he would not see death
before he had seen the Lord's Messiah.
Guided by the Spirit,
Simeon came into the Temple;
and when the parents brought in the child Jesus,
to do for him what was customary under the law,
Simeon took him in his arms
and praised God, saying,

"Master, now you are dismissing your servant in peace,
according to your word;
for my eyes have seen your Salvation,
which you have prepared in the presence
of all peoples,
a light for revelation to the Gentiles
and for glory to your people Israel."

And the child's father and mother were amazed
at what was being said about him.
Then Simeon blessed them
and said to his mother Mary,
"This child is destined for the falling
and the rising of many in Israel,
and to be a sign that will be opposed
so that the inner thoughts of many will be revealed—
and a sword will pierce your own soul, too."

There was also a prophet,
Anna the daughter of Phanuel,
of the tribe of Asher.
She was of great age,
having lived with her husband
seven years after her marriage,
then as a widow to the age of eighty-four.
She never left the Temple
but worshipped there with fasting and prayer,
night and day.
At that moment she came,
and began to praise God and to speak about the child
to all who were looking for the redemption of Israel.

Luke 2:22a, 25-38

THE WALK

The birth of Jesus brings about division for many. This most holy project announces promises to many for whom the world wants to cast aside or dismiss. Mary offers a prelude by her Magnificat, where she proclaims that the powerful will be cast down from their thrones and the lowly will be lifted up (Luke 1:46-55). Many, including both the poor and the wealthy, accept this promise, and we find that it is women who offer this path of transformation for us, first Mary, a young teen-age girl, and then Anna, 84 years old, who welcomes Jesus when he is presented in the Temple. Many—then and now—are threatened by such radical inclusion, a community consisting not only of women, but lepers, tax collectors, prostitutes, and offenders against the law. Today it is still women; those with same-sex orientation or differing cultural backgrounds, the young and the prisoner who scare us. Simeon foresees that Jesus is a light to all the nations. We are provoked and challenged to ask ourselves *Whose side are we on?*

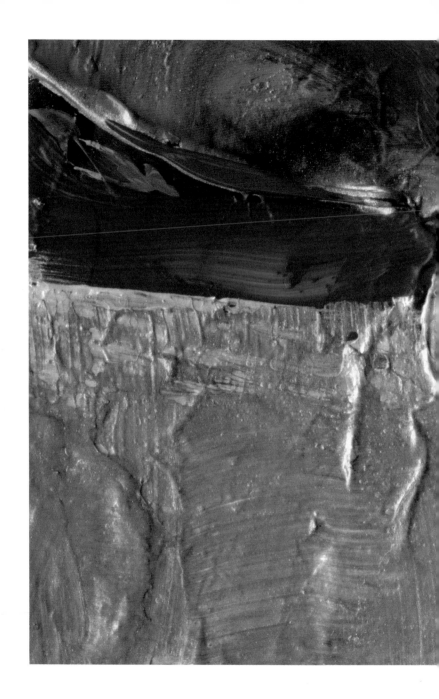

The Desert in Advent

THE TWELFTH STATION

The Flight into Egypt

THE WORD

An angel of the Lord
appeared to Joseph in a dream and said,
"Get up, take the child and his mother,
and flee to Egypt,
and remain there until I tell you;
for Herod is about to search for the child,
to destroy him."
Then Joseph got up,
took the child and his mother by night,
and went to Egypt,
and remained there until the death of Herod.
This was to fulfill what had been spoken
by the Lord through the prophet,
"Out of Egypt I have called my son."

Matthew 2:13-15

THE WALK

Our dreams can often serve as not only a moral compass, but also as a guide for discernment in our lives. Among all of the voices that invade our brains, perhaps it is in our dreams where we can, at times, receive the greatest wisdom. Our calling, in community, is to look out for one another, strengthen one another, and when necessary, protect one another in the most terrifying times. Our life of prayer calls us to not only hear, but listen to the voice of God, who is always prompting and guiding, leading and pulling us toward good decisions, often decisions that are for the welfare of another. Joseph is our model for such discernment, and he does so by his actions, because in Matthew's Gospel, Joseph never speaks a single word. He was humble enough to listen and not be swayed and, in the end, be guided by his fears or cultural bias. He pays attention to God's activity revealed in his dreams. Joseph truly leads by example, one that we are entrusted to carry on. We can see all around us, many who are wanderers, without direction and without a home. We are to "get up," and take on God's mission to serve and offer a balm of protection to those who are vulnerable. We need to listen, and then respond in action.

THE THIRTEENTH STATION

The Massacre of the Innocents

THE WORD

> When Herod saw that he had been tricked
> by the wise men,
> he was infuriated,
> and he sent for and killed all the children
> in and around Bethlehem
> who were two years old or under,
> according to the time that he had learned
> from the wise men.
>
> Then was fulfilled what had been spoken
> through the prophet Jeremiah:
> "A voice was heard in Ramah,
> wailing and loud lamentation,
> Rachel weeping for her children;
> She refused to be consoled,
> because they are no more."

Matthew 2:16-18

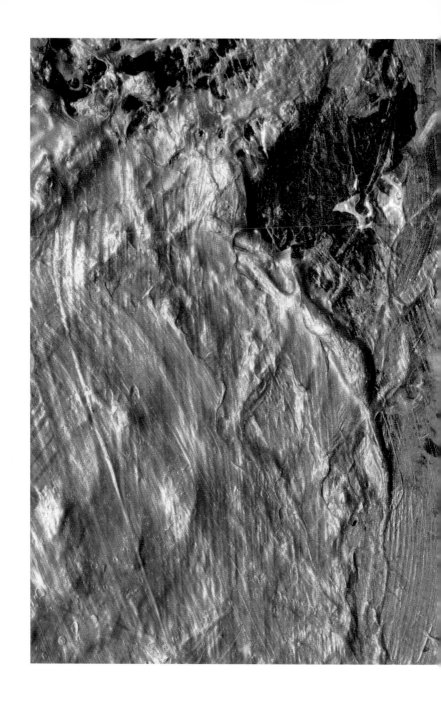

Emptied

THE WALK

This terrible and horrific story is one that we dare not try to escape. Like Rachel, the story itself cries out in lamentation, buried in despair. It is difficult and painful to contemplate this story in the midst of the good news of the birth of Jesus. The announcement of the Prince of Peace and the joy surrounding this news falls to the ground, giving way to fear, violence, danger and destruction. The lust for power is threatened, and so the threat needs to be neutralized. The result is that the joy of the Magi following the light of promise quickly becomes a raging song of anguish. We too often want to keep Christmas cozy, filled only with merriment and cheer. But the Son of God has entered a violent world. To embrace the birth of the Messiah is to be compelled to speak out against the demons of evil, especially those that harm our children. There are literally millions of children around the world who do not have access to clean and safe drinking water. Many of them are among the poorest of the poor, and are forced to consume contaminated food. Many are the helpless victims of physical and sexual abuse. If Herod appalls us, then we need to be equally appalled by how our own children are beaten and battered, enduring the most disgusting forms of suffering and death. First, we must lament, because by doing so, we are awakened to the horror. Only by taking this most difficult yet essential move, can we even think to rectify and heal our world.

Heart Coming Home

THE FOURTEENTH STATION

The Return to Nazareth

THE WORD

When Herod died,
an angel of the Lord suddenly appeared
in a dream to Joseph in Egypt and said,
"Get up, take the child and his mother,
and go to the land of Israel,
for those who were seeking the child's life are dead."
Then Joseph got up,
Took the child and his mother,
and went to the land of Israel.
But when he heard
that Archelaus was ruling over Judea
in place of his father Herod,
he was afraid to go there.
And after being warned in a dream,
he went away to the district of Galilee.
There he made his home in a town called Nazareth,
so that what had been spoken through the prophets
might be fulfilled,
"He will be called a Nazarene."

Matthew 2:19-23

THE WALK

No matter what the journey is, no matter where it takes us, no matter how long, coming home is always the place of wholeness. Home is where we want to ultimately end up, whether it is a place or being in the presence of those with whom we feel tethered. Home is usually a place of quiet, of simple living, of patterns that keep us connected to God and each other. To be born with Christ is about coming home to all things that are important. To let the Incarnation hold a precious space in our hearts means that we welcome all, care for all, and reach out to all who have no home. We will be pulled away from time to time, sometime for short amounts of time, and sometimes, for what may seem like an eternity away. So we are invited to consider going "home" from time to time, wherever it may be, and with whomever we choose to share it with. Each Christmas, every recognition of the Nativity calls us home, with Christ, who delivers, enlightens, guides, and shapes who we are: God's children.

WALK

WITH

CHRIST

**THE BIBLICAL WAY OF THE
CROSS WITH THE GOSPELS**

> Look to Christ to be your light; follow.
> Leave behind your former self and live.
> Don't look back, don't be afraid; follow.
> Come to Christ, walk with Christ, and live.[2]

The ancient tradition of praying the Way of the Cross has been an important and rich practice for Christians throughout history. The ritual pattern of remembering, retracing, and walking the Passion and Death of Jesus continues to this day to be a most revered and sacred keeping of this central mystery of our life of faith.

In 1991, Saint John Paul II began a new way for us to think about the "stations" of the Cross, that is more authentically in line with what we find in the New Testament, and also consistent with the most ancient practice of this devotional prayer form. Some of the traditional stations that do not actually appear in Scripture were dropped (such as the three falls of Jesus, the meeting with his mother, the encounter with Veronica), and important scenes were reinstated, as they were and still too often tend to be, overlooked: Jesus' prayer in the Garden of Olives, the betrayal of Judas, Peter's denial, the judgment of Pilate, the scourging, the promise made to the good thief, and Jesus' words to this mother and the beloved disciple at the foot of the Cross.

One may notice that, for the "walk" reflections found in these stations, the term *Christ* is used instead of the more human or historical name, *Jesus*. This distinction is intended, so that when we observe the Way of the Cross, we look not only at what scholars would call the "Pre-Easter" Jesus, but that we would also challenge ourselves to consider and reflect upon the "Post-Easter" Jesus, who is the Christ who lives and breathes and moves and acts in our lives right here, and right now; over and over again. In other words, it is my hope that praying with this pattern, we would be able to call upon and speak to and with a living Christ, who transcends his historical life on the earth. As I paraphrased 2 Corinthians 4:10 years ago in one of my early liturgical songs:

> We hold the death of the Lord deep in our hearts.
> Living, now we remain with Jesus the Christ.[3]

May we in this ritual pattern of walking with Christ, take up our Cross, and come to know the Lord more deeply as both Jesus *and* Christ.

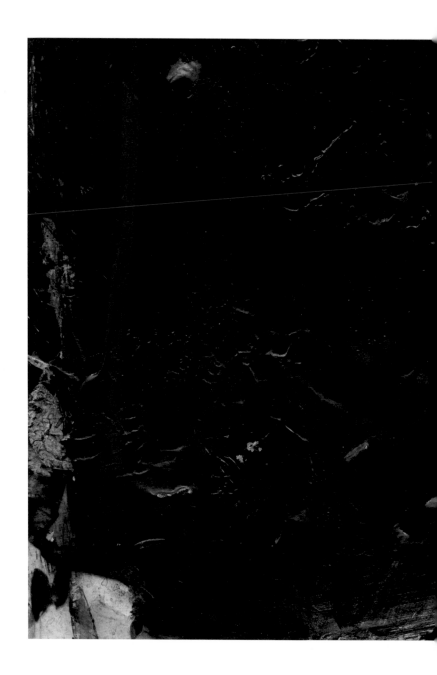

Gethsemane

THE FIRST STATION

Jesus Prays in the Garden of Olives

THE WORD

Jesus came out and went, as was his custom,
to the Mount of Olives;
and the disciples followed him.
When he reached the place, he said to them,
"Pray that you may not come into the time of trial."
Then he withdrew from them about a stone's throw,
knelt down, and prayed,
"Father if you are willing, remove this cup from me,
yet not my will but yours be done."

Then an angel from heaven appeared to him and
gave him strength.
In his anguish he prayed more earnestly,
and his sweat became like great drops of blood
falling down on the ground.
When he got up from prayer,
he came to the disciples and found them sleeping

because of grief, and he said to them,
"Why are you sleeping?
Get up and pray that you may not come into
the time of trial."

Luke 22:39-46

THE WALK

As we love life and fear death, so did Christ. As the disciples were anxious and afraid, so was Christ. The example given is an invitation to pray in whatever garden we find ourselves. And we do so when prayer seems all but impossible, in the darkest and most horrific times and seasons. But we pray. While we find ourselves in the dark, dank, and lonely place of solitude, we remember that we really are not alone. When it seems as if the song is absent, there is music in the garden. For gardens are places where things grow. For Christ, this garden was a place of pain, betrayal and looming death. For us, it may be the same at the moment, but we know it is not the last word. We have to go there, we must embrace the terror of this moment and not try to cheat it, or walk around it and escape. We must, as Christ did, walk *through* it. This is not a prayer we want to pray. But this is a prayer that we must attend to. Otherwise, the trembling of our lives will never move forward, and we will linger in anguish. Time in the garden is necessary. Good things will grow there watered by our tears.

THE SECOND STATION

Jesus is Betrayed by Judas

The Word

> Then he came to the disciples and said to them,
> "Are you still sleeping and taking your rest?
> See, the hour is at hand,
> and the Son of Man is betrayed into the hands
> of sinners.
> Get up, let us be going.
> See, my betrayer is at hand!"
>
> While he was still speaking,
> Judas, one of the twelve, arrived;
> with him was a large crowd with swords and clubs,
> from the chief priests and the elders of the people.
> Now the betrayer had given them a sign, saying,
> "The one I will kiss is the man; arrest him."
> At once he came up to Jesus and said,
> "Greetings, Rabbi!" and kissed him.

Matthew 26:45-49

I Know Who You Are

THE WALK

We all know the crushing pain of betrayal. So did Christ. From our time as young children through to our aging years, we trust and we surrender so much to others: our confidences, our hopes, our deepest joys and darkest secrets—the most vulnerable corners of our lives. As we get older our ability to trust weakens. It is difficult to know who or where our friends and advocates are, and when we are honest with ourselves, we also know how we can be perpetrators ourselves, who damage and poison the most sacred of relationships. Christ knew this. Christ knows this. And the response of Christ is always the same, that even in the darkest moments of abandonment and humiliation, the response is always to *love*. If we are truly ambassadors of God, witnesses of the presence of Christ, then we too are called to summon up the strength to respond in the same way in the midst of our betrayed hearts—with love. To be obedient to the way of Christ is to love. To not do so is to betray Christ.

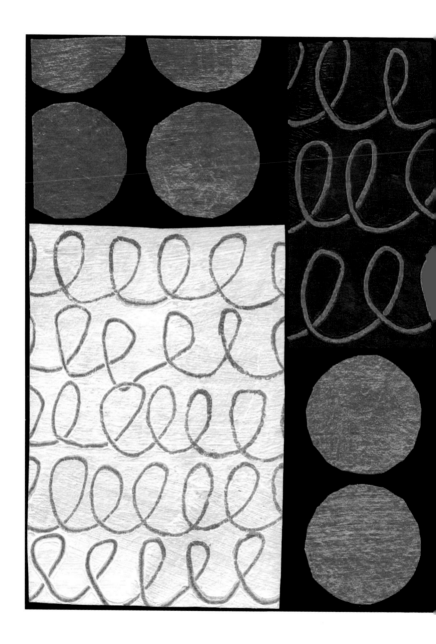

Taxing Questions

THE THIRD STATION

Jesus is Condemned to Death by the Sanhedrin

THE WORD

For many gave false testimony against him,
and their testimony did not agree.
Again, the high priest asked him,
"Are you the Messiah, the Son of the Blessed One?"
Jesus said, "I am;
and 'you will see the Son of Man seated
at the right hand of the Power,'
and 'coming with the clouds of heaven.'"

Then the high priest tore his clothes and said,
"Why do we still need witnesses?
You have heard the blasphemy!
What is your decision?"
All of them condemned him as deserving death.

Mark 14:56, 61-64

THE WALK

To receive unjust judgment and condemnation from those who hold power is a mark that is very difficult to erase. We all know the embarrassment, the anger and rage, and how self-destructive behaviors and voices in our heads can flood our psyches. It may be difficult to realize this, but so did Christ. Christ, who was called to lead his people, was hated, despised and punished for such leadership, by both the religious and political "leaders" of his time. They did not embrace his leadership—they sought to destroy it, by destroying him through his life and blood. When we seek to "lead" and serve with the heart and mind of Christ, we too receive the pain of hatred and, at times, feel criminalized for doing so. Because to follow Christ, and to lead as Christ leads, is a path that our world, our politics, and even our Church have difficult times swallowing. Because the way of Christ is love, peace, justice, mercy, forgiveness and lifting up the poorest of the poor and holding high hope and freedom that these other forces cannot provide, or even care to. We have to sit in this, to realize that to walk this walk, condemnation is bound to follow.

THE FOURTH STATION

Jesus is Denied by Peter

THE WORD

They seized him and led him away,
bringing him into the high priest's house.
But Peter was following at a distance.
When they had kindled a fire in the middle of the
courtyard
and sat down together,
Peter sat among them.
Then a servant-girl, seeing him in the firelight,
stared at him and said, "This man also was with him."
But he denied it, saying, "Woman, I do not know him."
A little later someone else, on seeing him, said,
"You also are one of them."
But Peter said, "Man, I am not!"

Then about an hour later, still another kept insisting,
"Surely this man also was with him; for he is a Galilean."
But Peter said,
"Man, I do not know what you are talking about!"
At that moment, while he was still speaking,
the cock crowed.

Holy Absence

The Lord turned and looked at Peter.
Then Peter remembered the word of the Lord,
how he said to him,
"Before the cock crows today, you will deny me
three times."
And he went out and wept bitterly.

Luke 22: 54-62

THE WALK

When a dear friend abandons and denies who we are,
when they deny the best in ourselves, reject our finest
moments and actions, we can find ourselves unable
to breathe, bringing about sadness too heavy to carry.
Christ carried this burden, not only by the rejection of
Peter, but from all of his friends and companions. Christ
felt the pain of being and feeling very much alone. We
all know the pain of being the victim of such denial,
but we can be deniers as well. We deny the very best in
our friends, clinging to resentment and seeking revenge;
and we even deny our very selves. We deny the bless-
edness that our very birth guarantees for us through
self-destructive choices and attitudes. When we commit
these actions—toward others and toward ourselves—we
deny Christ. We deny Christ when we are indifferent to
suffering; we deny Christ when we are not truly present
to the varied particles of another's life; we deny Christ
when we are complacent in seeking to change systems
that steal and poison the lives of our people. We must
not run the other way. Rather, we must act. We must
speak. We must live what is true.

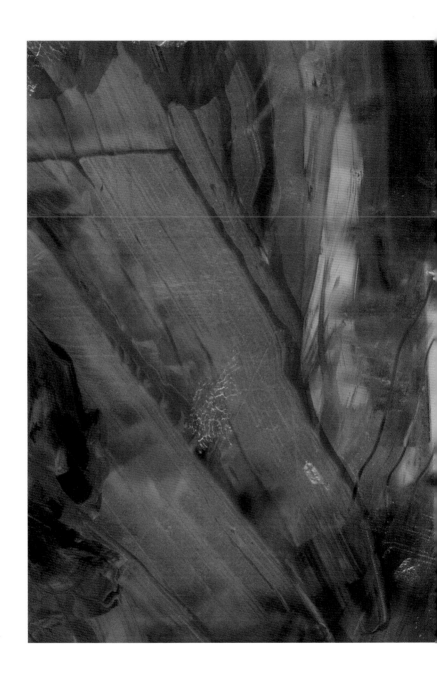

Gathering Courage

THE FIFTH STATION

Jesus is Judged by Pilate

THE WORD

Pilate, wanting to release Jesus, addressed them again;
but they kept shouting,
"Cruficy, crucify him!"
A third time he said to them,
"Why, what evil has he done?
I have found in him no ground for the sentence of death;
I will, therefore, have him flogged and then
release him."

But they kept urgently demanding with loud shouts
that he should be crucified, and their voices prevailed.
So Pilate gave his verdict
that their demand should be granted.
He released the man they asked for,
the one who had been put in prison for insurrection
and murder,
and he handed over Jesus as they wished.

Luke 23:20-25

THE WALK

The saying, "To thine own self be true," is a most difficult adage to live by because to do so means we must remain faithful to who and what God created us to be. Christ did surrender himself to those in power without resistance, but he never surrendered the very core of himself. That would be to deny his destiny. To gain his life, to retain and strengthen and amplify who he was and is, Christ had to be willing to give it all up, and allow others to control the outcome. This is the way of looking ahead to carry the Cross. We have to be willing to lose everything in order to receive and accept the glorious gift of life to the full. The things we hold the most precious—we must be open to handing them over, totally, completely. Christ taught peace in a culture of fear, war and suspicion. We live and try to breathe in and out, a goodness that the world often wants to tear down and destroy. We need to put on Christ, and resist the lure to return evil with evil, and walk the way of mercy, forgiveness, and love. With no strings attached.

THE SIXTH STATION

Jesus is Scourged and Crowned with Thorns

THE WORD

Then Pilate took Jesus and had him flogged.
And the soldiers wove a crown of thorns
and put it on his head,
and they dressed him in a purple robe.
They kept coming up to him, saying,
"Hail, King of the Jews!"
and striking him on the face.

John 19:1-3

THE WALK

The rage of violence is so pervasive in our world that we can become numbed to the horror of it all. It is everywhere—in our world, in our neighborhoods, and yes, even in our Church. At times, it is graphic and unapolo-

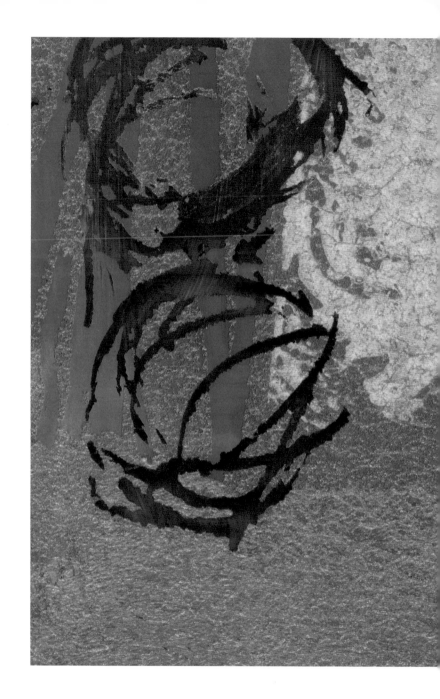

Holy Even in Pain

getic, and at other times, it is subtle and sinister. But it is here, all around us. We do not have to look far to find it. But remember, Christ was not only fully Divine, but also, fully human: fragile, frightened, and in this setting, the very victim of hatred and abuse beyond description. But we do not have to look only toward this story in the Scriptures because the story continually plays itself out in our world, and we take part in it, sometimes directly, physically, or psychologically, or by our indifference and carelessness. We scourge each other and destroy so much in each other to the extent that we often forget to pause and consider what we are doing. We scourge the poor and the homeless; we flog the hungry and lonely; we place crowns of thorns on those different than ourselves, those whom we judge to be less or even immoral. There are too many ways to mention how we choose to do this to the Body of Christ. But we can choose differently.

Good Friday

THE SEVENTH STATION

Jesus Carries His Cross

THE WORD

So they took Jesus;
And carrying the Cross by himself,
he went out to what is called
The Place of the Skull,
which in Hebrew is called Golgotha.

John 19:17

THE WALK

Far too many among us live and walk a journey that is, most of the time, filled with nothing but darkness, sadness and grief. The desperation of many is the same desperation and ache that Christ had to face, not only at this moment, but still to this day for so many who have to carry a daily cross of loneliness, hunger, home-lessness, anxiety, depression, addiction, discrimination, and the deepest persecution for who they are, for who they choose to and are called to love. We live in hope because we are given the example of Christ, who walked the life of the cross with courage, strength, and deep faith that he was not alone. His "Abba" ("Daddy") was with him every step of the way. So it is for us, and we do so by walking with the Cross in every aspect of our lives: to bear with one another, serving those who dwell in poverty, by welcoming in those whom are the outcast, and pulling closer to us those who are on the outside of life. Christ is our strength and hope, and his "Abba" is our protection. It is our call to follow.

THE EIGHTH STATION

Jesus is Helped by Simon of Cyrene

THE WORD

After mocking him,
they stripped him of the purple cloak
and put his own clothes on him.
Then they led him out to crucify him.
They compelled a passer-by,
who was coming in from the country,
to carry his cross;
it was Simon of Cyrene,
the father of Alexander and Rufus.

Mark 15:20-21

THE WALK

Generosity. Going out of one's way. Inconveniencing
oneself for another. Self-sacrifice. Becoming and living

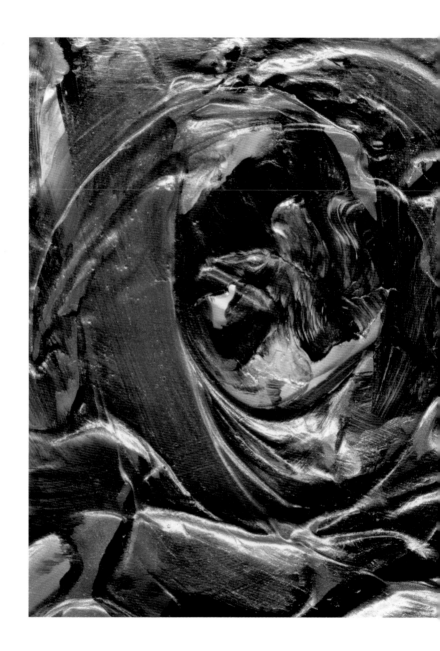

The Hospitality of Mercy

the compassionate life. It is this simple. While we carry the burden of our own cross, we are moved to remember our sisters and brothers who hold their own burdens, troubles and deep anxiety. We walk with them, not just when we are doing well, but rather, alongside and in the midst of our own brokenness, pain and suffering. To follow Christ is to follow the way of lavish generosity that not only helps, but also heals. To follow Christ is to be attentive, to be "present" to those far away, and very close by, who are crying and aching for help. Beyond reaching to friends and strangers in need, we are also all in need of asking, receiving and welcoming in such help for ourselves. We do not walk this journey alone. We lift and hold each other up. We reach out with our minds, our hands, and our hearts. And to the extent that we are open to doing so, for each other and for ourselves, our own cross will be that much lighter.

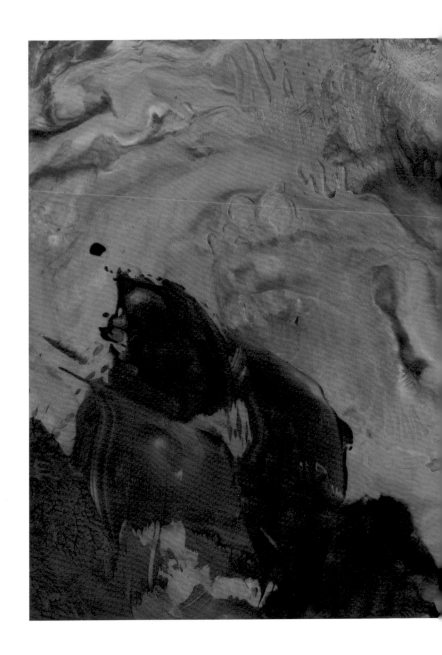

Gift of Longing

THE NINTH STATION

Jesus Encounters the Women of Jerusalem

THE WORD

A great number of the people followed him,
and among them were women
who were beating their breasts and wailing for him.
But Jesus turned to them and said,
"Daughters of Jerusalem, do not weep for me,
but weep for yourselves and for your children.
For the days are surely coming when they will say,
'Blessed are the barren, and the wombs that
never bore,
and the breasts that never nursed.'
Then they will begin to say to the mountains,
'Fall on us'; and to the hills, 'Cover us.'
For if they do this when the wood is green,
what will happen when it is dry?"

Luke 23:27-31

THE WALK

Most certainly, women understand pain. Christ knew this. We know this. Women throughout the Hebrew and Christian Testaments help us to confront grief and pain, and the loss and possibilities of new life and birth. Not only the daughters of Jerusalem, but also the daughters of our own time beat their breasts and wail tears of pain for their children, for the destruction of life, for the sin of hunger and homelessness and the horror of abuse and domestic violence. They give witness to the message of Christ. They offer testimony for us of the way of the cross that we are all called to carry. Their canticles and laments help us to pray, sing, cry out, rejoice, and dance with the utmost abandon the revelation of resurrection and hope. Women of faith have always planted footprints for all of us to follow. We should ponder the memories and presence of women in our lives who help us to be like Christ, who provide for us a lens to see more clearly the ironic gift of lament, song and cry that can truly set us free.

THE TENTH STATION

Jesus is Crucified

THE WORD

Then they brought Jesus to the place called Golgotha
(which means the place of the skull),
and they offered him wine mixed with myrrh;
but he did not take it.

And they crucified him,
and divided his clothes among them,
casting lots to decide what each should take.
It was nine o'clock in the morning when they
crucified him.
The inscription of the charge against him read,
"The King of the Jews."

Mark 15:22-26

The Shape He Makes

THE WALK

It is so difficult to let go, to surrender with total faith and understanding that we will be able to survive, sometimes, let alone flourish. Christ was able to do this. This witness of Christ we can see in the lives of Saints, with others who belong to the "cloud of witnesses," and among many whom we know well, the dead and the living among us. Christ knew the cost. It was for him, and is for us, clear and resolute. To live the life of faith means to walk to the edge of the cliff, and take one more step. Christ laughs and cries with us, and walks the lonely roads that we encounter. When we see others in the midst of deep pain and suffering, we need to remember, these poor ones are Christ. When we experience our own failures and demons, we need to recall, that Christ is right here sinking in the quicksand with us. Christ was executed for disrupting the status quo of hatred and corrupt empire. He did not shrink from his association with his God, or with God's cause. Christ lived the radical life. We are called to respond, to really try to live and serve one another with this same lavish and radical love.

Where Hope Lives

THE ELEVENTH STATION

Jesus Promises to Share His Reign with the Good Thief

THE WORD

One of the criminals who were hanged there
kept deriding him and saying,
"Are you not the Messiah? Save yourself and us."
But the other rebuked him, saying,
"Do you not fear God,
since you are under the same sentence of
condemnation?
And we, indeed, have been condemned justly,
for we are getting what we deserve for our deeds,
but this man has done nothing wrong."

Then he said,
"Jesus, remember me when you come into your
kingdom."
He replied,
"Truly I tell you,
today you will be with me in Paradise."

Luke 23:39-43

THE WALK

Christ always chooses to see our best selves. He does not (and will not) haunt us with our sins, for the love of Christ is greater than all of the demons that dwell in and among us. We are given more chances than we deserve, and we are constantly being loved into a new day, each and every day, no matter our sin, no matter how heinous our actions can be, no matter how awful we treat one another or even, ourselves. This love keeps on coming, as Christ sees and wants only beautiful things in us. If we believe that in community, we are the Body of Christ, then we are to see, love, and celebrate the very best in each other that we see, or perhaps have not yet discovered. Christ poured out his blood, and we are called to make a similar oblation, to offer love to one another, and especially to those whom we find difficult to love. That is what the reign of God is all about—it is about sharing good news, new life and renewed hope to all who seem to only know or inflict bad news, darkness, cynicism and hopelessness. To follow and become Christ is to become a home for all—especially those who are cast aside and seem lost.

THE TWELFTH STATION

Jesus Speaks to Mary and the Beloved Disciple at the Foot of the Cross

THE WORD

Meanwhile,
standing near the cross of Jesus were his mother,
and his mother's sister, Mary the wife of Clopas,
and Mary Magdalene.
When Jesus saw his mother
and the disciple whom he loved standing beside her,
he said to his mother, "Woman, here is your son."
Then he said to the disciple, "Here is your mother."
And from that hour
the disciple took her into his own home.

John 19:25-27

Remembering Forward

THE WALK

To take up the cross means to lose and offer up the "self" and, in turn, offer and turn over our very selves to and for one another. This is what Christ asks of us. The ache for community, the longing to belong is strong for all of us. This yearning rises in both introverts as well as extroverts, and the human need to cling to each other is not weakness at all. Rather, it is to live in line with God's covenant, and the call of Christ to take in sons and daughters, mothers and fathers, friends and companions in order to keep moving; to live on and take up the daily crosses that make up both the terror and gift of life. In the most basic of terms, we need to be attentive to one another, watch over each other, and keep each other safe. We can do this. But we cannot do it alone. We need each other, and we need to keep Christ, our brother and friend, by our side as we take up this charge. If we keep watch, stay open, trust deeply, love lavishly, and serve passionately, we will be more deeply connected to each other, and closer to Christ.

Good Friday II

THE THIRTEENTH STATION

Jesus Dies on the Cross

THE WORD

From noon on,
darkness came over the whole land
until three in the afternoon.
And at about three o'clock Jesus cried with a loud voice,
"Eli, Eli, lema sabachthani?" that is,
"My God, my God, why have you forsaken me?"
When some of the bystanders heard it, they said,
"This man is calling for Elijah."

At once, one of them ran and got a sponge,
filled it with sour wine, put it on a stick,
and gave it to him to drink.
But the others said,
"Wait, let us see whether Elijah will come to save him."
Then Jesus cried again with a loud voice
and breathed his last.

Matthew 27:45-50

THE WALK

Our faith is grounded in the *belief* that Christ is with us, always. But our *experience* often seems to proclaim that far too often, Christ seems very absent. To be in the presence of death, is a very lonely and desperate reality. Death is everywhere, and no matter what we may concoct in the many efforts to delay or cheat it, every one of us one day, will die. Some of us will go to the other side peacefully, others of us, tragically. Some of us will face this mystery with acceptance, and others of us will go down kicking and screaming. But it is a reality that we all face. To live in the Paschal Mystery—the life, deeds, death and resurrection of Jesus—we are to courageously accept this walk of life with eyes wide open as to where it will eventually lead us. We hold the death of the Lord deep in our hearts. But now, and in the reign of God, we are and will be living, remaining with this Christ who gave of himself, who intentionally accepted the reality of being broken and poured out. *This* is love beyond love, pain for our pain. So we take this step with Christ, discovering once again that he alone is the source of all that we love, live, long and die for.

THE FOURTEENTH STATION

Jesus is Placed in the Tomb

THE WORD

When it was evening,
there came a rich man from Arimathea, named Joseph,
who was also a disciple of Jesus.
He went to Pilate and asked for the body of Jesus;
then Pilate ordered it to be given to him.

So Joseph took the body
and wrapped it in a clean linen cloth
and laid it in his own new tomb,
which he had hewn in rock.
He then rolled a great stone to the door of the tomb
and went away.
Mary Magdalene and the other Mary were there,
sitting opposite the tomb.

Matthew 27:57-61

Into Earth

THE WALK

The journey of Christ's walk and way toward death beckons us to connect this big story to a smaller, albeit, still an important story—ours. We live the entirety of our lives collecting, hoarding, and sustaining so much. Much of it good, too much of it perhaps bad, but all of it, tells the story of *who* we are. At the hour of our death, we confront *whose* we are. We are one with Christ. We belong to Christ. And we are buried with Christ, and with everything that we bring with us to the tomb. Many people who face death see their life "flashing before their eyes" with full memory, and for those who cannot remember it all; they still carry it with them in the very depths of their being. It certainly was the case for Christ. It certainly is the case for us. We do more than die; we also bury with us all of the stuff and baggage of our lives, and that will always stay in the ground or in the ashes of our entombment. We seek to remember the various chapters of our life, but we do more than that. We celebrate these chapters, and believe that we will rise above and beyond it all.

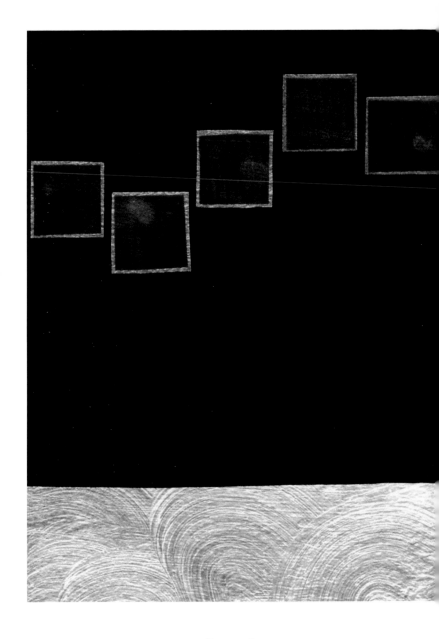

Resurrection

THE FIFTEENTH STATION

Jesus is Raised from the Dead

THE WORD

On the first day of the week, at early dawn,
they came to the tomb,
taking the spices that they had prepared.
They found the stone rolled away from the tomb,
but when they went in, they did not find the body.

Luke 24:1-3

THE WALK

We *believe* and *preach* Christ crucified, but the Christ that
we *follow*, is the Risen Lord, the Christ that transcends
his specific human story in history, always moving well
beyond the circumstances and narratives of his passion
and death. We sing and cry out, celebrating an empty
tomb, and are called to free each other and ourselves
from the tombs that we sometimes cling to because to

truly live in the light of the *Risen* Christ may seem even more terrifying. We need to break out of what is often a *comfort* of our tombs, and make daily choices to really live, to truly, as Thoreau said, "suck the marrow out of life." We choose life, not death. We choose joy over sadness. We choose to revel in the empowering promise of Christ, not the empty promise of the "Satans" that want to hinder and devour us. We choose to live passionately, not with apathy and indifference. We choose to serve rather than be served. We choose to increase and lift up another person's life rather than our own. We choose a humility that is not grounded in what can ironically become an arrogant sense of self-hatred, but one that, with an investment that is total, that leans and surrenders to the love of God that will never let us go. We choose to rise.

RISE

===========

WITH

===========

CHRIST

===========

THE WAY OF THE RESURRECTION
WITH THE NEW TESTAMENT

> The tomb is empty, is empty!
> Go and serve all people who long to be free!
> Raise those who sleep,
> who sleep in tombs of fear,
> and give them eyes to see!
> Sing Alleluia![4]

The Gospel story certainly does not end with the Passion and Death of Christ, if we truly embrace the Paschal Mystery as central to our lives as Christians. Every thing we do as a Church points toward Easter and its implications, consequences, and the risks that it asks of us. The empty tomb and the promises that it holds are central. Easter is not just Easter Sunday. It is a season, a call to fifty days of unceasing rejoicing. This is, of course, difficult for us to hold because of how the season of Easter rubs shoulders with what every spring brings in both the world and in the Church. It is almost impossible to sustain a buoyant joy in our liturgical life that can bridge the community from the Easter Vigil to Pentecost and beyond.

Rise with Christ is a journey, a tethering together of 15 stations that hopefully continue to unpack what this season, or more importantly, this central fixture of our faith holds. It is an adaptation of a practice that actually began in 1994, known as the Stations of Light, or also called, *Via Lucis* (Latin for "The Way of Light"). I have added the fifteenth station, which honors the conversion of Paul, as truly a Resurrection event.

The victory of the Resurrection truly gives meaning and hope to the pain and terror of life. It is my hope that this "way" of keeping the Easter season, will enrich and deepen the joy of the empty tomb in the reality of our lives.

THE FIRST STATION

Risen

THE WORD

On the first day of the week, at early dawn,
they came to the tomb, taking the spices they had
prepared.
They found the stone rolled away from the tomb,
but when they went in,
the did not find the body.
While they were perplexed about this,
suddenly two men in dazzling clothes
stood beside them.
The women were terrified
and bowed their faces to the ground,
but the men said to them,
"Why do you look for the living among the dead?
He is not here, but has risen.
Remember how he told you,
while he was still in Galilee,
that the Son of Man must be handed over to sinners,
and be crucified,
and on the third day rise again."

Risen

They remembered his words,
and returning from the tomb,
they told all this to the eleven and to all the rest.

Luke 24:1-9

THE WALK

We need to keep reminding ourselves that our ways are
not the ways of God. God's ways are far above and beyond
what we can ever hope to understand. God's ways are the
ways of the impossible, and that is why these are holy
things, because they are not the work of our hands. We
keep looking for life among things that no longer breathe.
We cling to the graves of things that have long since died,
of ideas, visions and that which we hope will remain living, as long as we hold on tight enough. We do not want
those close to us to change and grow, so we try to control
them. It is easier to stay tethered to those things that
we know, deep down, are dead. It is safer that way. The
messengers are speaking to us today, teaching us that
we need to stop living in death, and move forward to a
new day. But these two ambassadors of new life remind
us that resurrection is still connected to the real world,
inviting and provoking us to live as Christ, living lives of
generous hospitality, of healing, and courage in standing
up to systems that the powerful use and abuse for causes
not of God. This empty tomb breaks the silence, shouting
to all who will hear and listen, challenging us to truly
live, to speak truth, and become resurrection to all who
dwell in the darkness. The women here remembered this
truth, and it roused their commitment. This same coura-
geous response is asked of us.

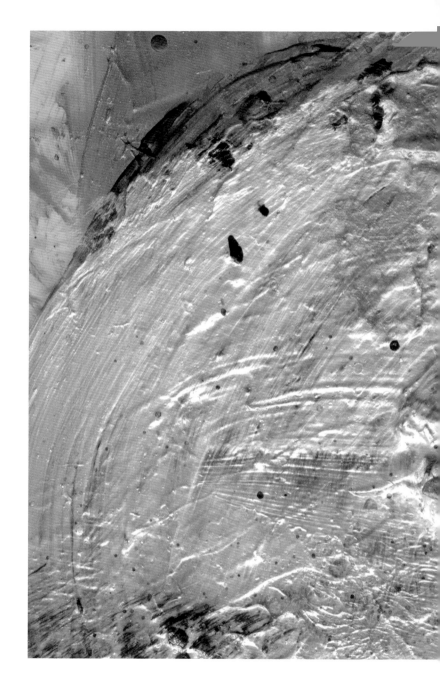

I Do Not Know Where They Have Laid Him

THE SECOND STATION

Empty Tomb

THE WORD

Mary Magdalene ran and went to Simon Peter
and the other disciple, the one whom Jesus loved,
and said to them,
"They have taken the Lord out of the tomb,
and we do not know where they have laid him."
Then Peter and the other disciple set out
and went toward the tomb.
The two were running together,
but the other disciple outran Peter
and reached the tomb first.
He bent down to look in
and saw the linen wrappings lying there,
but did not go in.
Then Simon Peter came,
Saw the linen wrappings lying there,
And the cloth that had been on Jesus' head,
not lying with the linen wrappings
but rolled up in a place by itself.

> Then the other disciple,
> who reached the tomb first, also went in,
> and he saw and believed;
> for as yet they did not understand the scripture,
> that he must rise from the dead.
> Then the disciples returned to their homes.

John 20:1-10

THE WALK

The disciple whom Jesus loved arrives first at the tomb, and is the first to believe. He moves without hesitation, breathless and anxious to see hope and joy restored. We know people like this. Maybe we are like this. We see with almost naïve optimism, possibilities for generosity and service, believing without reserve that life always conquers death. We can refuse to face facts as most would see, and we cheerlead others on and we draw courage ourselves from their sometimes impulsive actions of hope. Peter? Well, he runs. Always moving without thinking, but always with passion. His running now is not away from Jesus, as he did the previous few days, but now, *toward* Jesus. We know people like this. Maybe we are like this. We boast and then deny. We are loyal, then not so loyal. We can become threatened in some way, and so we leave. But just as quickly, we can truly turn around, piercing through our jealousies of others who seem so blessed and confident. We can confess our sins, our shortcomings, and recognize and name the demons to see that new life is what we seek, and we hope to catch yet another glimpse of what is promised for us. We believe. We run. We live.

THE THIRD STATION

Mary Magdalene

THE WORD

She turned around and saw Jesus standing there,
but she did not know that it was Jesus.
Jesus said to her,
"Woman, why are you weeping?
Whom are you looking for?"
Supposing him to be the gardener,
she said to him,
"Sir, if you have carried him away,
tell me where you have laid him,
and I will take him away."
Jesus said to her, "Mary!"
She returned and said to him in Hebrew,
"Rabbouni!" (which means Teacher).

Mary Magdalene went and announced to the disciples,
"I have seen the Lord."

John 20:14-16, 18a

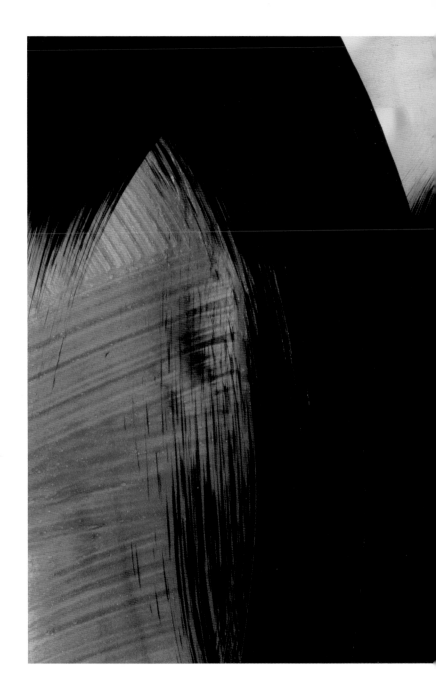

And Love Will Rise Up and Call Us By Name

THE WALK

Mary Magdalene speaks. She comes to mourn the loss of life, and her grief practically cripples her. Her thinking is not clear, and coming closer to the tomb feels like it will soon become hers. Then she is called by her name, and she responds without hesitation or reservation, "Teacher!" Jesus commissions her and her response is joyful obedience, knowing that she cannot cling to what she is seeing at this moment. She must leave the garden and tell the news of what she has witnessed. Like her, we are all called by name; we are all being commissioned. If all we do is linger and gaze on paranormal things, and remain drunk in the visions and moments of glory, then new life will not rise up. We are called to shout and live with all of our passion and energy, that death is not in charge. We weep, but we cling to the belief that one day, we will laugh. We mourn and are sick with grief, but we hang on with everything we have, believing that healing and restoration is real and promised for us. She has seen the Lord. And we see the Lord as well, in the promises fulfilled and risings made real. Thank God that Mary speaks. Because of her response, we can find our own voice. We then, will and do, see the Lord.

Emmaus

THE FOURTH STATION

Emmaus

THE WORD

Now on that same day two of them
were going to a village called Emmaus,
about seven miles from Jerusalem,
and talking with each other
about all these things that had happened.
While they were talking and discussing,
Jesus himself came near and went with them,
but their eyes were kept from recognizing him.
And he said to them,
"What are you discussing with each other
while you walk along?"
They stood still, looking sad.
Then one of them, whose name was Cleopas,
answered him,
"Are you the only stranger in Jerusalem
who does not know the things
that have taken place there in these days?"
He asked them, "What things?"

They replied,
"The things about Jesus of Nazareth,
 who was a prophet mighty in deed and word
before God and all the people,
and how our chief priests and leaders
handed him over to be condemned to death
and crucified him.
But we had hoped that he was the one to redeem
Israel.
Yes, and besides all this,
it is now the third day since these things took place.
Moreover, some women of our group astounded us.
They were at the tomb early this morning,
and when they did not find his body there,
they came back and told us
that they had indeed seen a vision of angels
who said that he was alive.
Some of those who were with us went to the tomb
and found it just as the women had said;
but they did not see him."
Then he said to them,
"Oh, how foolish you are,
and how slow of heart to believe all
that the prophets have declared!
Was it not necessary that the Messiah
should suffer these things and then enter into
his glory?"
Then beginning with Moses and all the prophets,
he interpreted to them the things about himself in
all the scriptures.

Luke 24: 13-27

THE WALK

We feel as though we have ransomed our lives and commitments to the wrong voice. So what do we do in our despair and cynicism? We head back to our ordinary tasks and routines, our work and our broken lives. It seems as though the "Alleluia's" previously sung have been a mistake. Death and suffering still seems to surround and at times, choke us. Our questions and conversations with important or even new relationships try to make sense out of some very powerful and hopeful things, things that seem to have been sucked into space. We feel helpless: "...we had hoped that he was the one...." We stay stuck in conversations that will keep us hopelessly moving in circles of doubt, discouragement and fear. We need to stop talking and processing the same things so much, and start listening to the story of God's agenda and program for our lives. We are hungering for something to believe in, to hope for. Perhaps the answer for our ache and thirst is found when we open our hearts and minds to let the stranger or unlikely person in, to guide us to see life in the here and now. The risk to speak to, or welcome in the stranger is real, but the possibility of taking the leap can restore and save our lives.

And Open Our Eyes to Behold Love's Face

THE FIFTH STATION

The Breaking of the Bread

THE WORD

As they came near the village to which they were going,
he walked ahead as if he were going on.
But they urged him strongly, saying,
"Stay with us, because it is almost evening
and the day is now nearly over."
So he went in to stay with them.
When he was at the table with them,
he took bread, blessed and broke it,
and gave it to them.
Then their eyes were opened,
and they recognized him;
and he vanished from their sight.
They said to each other,
"Were not our hearts burning within us
while he was talking to us on the road,
while he was opening the scriptures to us?"
That same hour they got up and returned to Jerusalem;
and they found the eleven and their companions

gathered together.
They were saying, "The Lord has risen indeed,
and he has appeared to Simon!"
Then they told what had happened on the road,
and how he had been made known to them
in the breaking of the bread.

Luke 24: 28-35

THE WALK

Whenever we experience real signs of rising taking place, we always want more. When conversations take place that transform, we want to linger so we can see and taste more. When we are at table, when we break the bread and share in sacred meals and encounters, we not only reach our true destination but are also given a new itinerary to follow. Once we were weary travelers, but now we feel alive and ready to move. In the breaking and sharing in the feast, the empty tomb is something we can taste and be sustained by. In the breaking of the bread, our burning hearts can become a fire to serve, seeking to build and feed upon and feed others in the sacred meal of resurrection. Burning hearts can open more blinded hearts, and heal broken hearts. Christ is that burning presence, that most sacred and bountiful meal of understanding, of recognition, of transformation, of becoming what we eat. Bread shared leads to resurrection. Breaking this bread means that it is for all. That is the destination. Not Emmaus. Not even Jerusalem. But rather, the lives and hopes of all, the Body of Christ.

THE SIXTH STATION

Appearing

THE WORD

While they were talking about this,
Jesus himself stood among them and said to them,
"Peace be with you."
They were startled and terrified,
and thought that they were seeing a ghost.
He said to them,
"Why are you frightened,
and why do doubts arise in your hearts?
Look at my hands and my feet;
see that it is I myself.
Touch me and see;
for a ghost does not have flesh
and bones as you see that I have."
And when he had said this,
he showed them his hands and his feet.
While in their joy they were disbelieving
and still wondering, he said to them,
"Have you anything here to eat?"

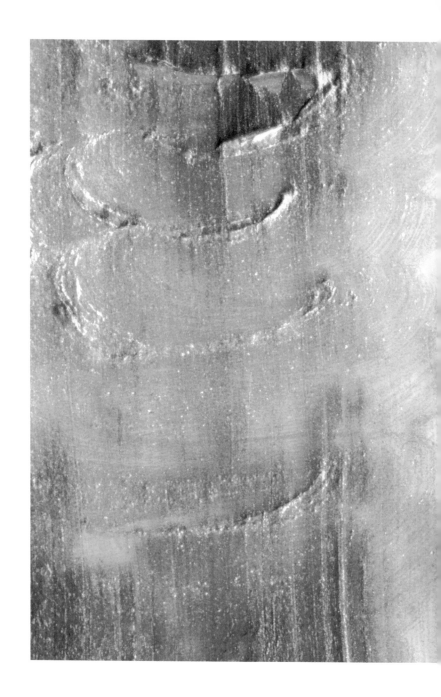

All It Can Say Is Holy

They gave him a piece of broiled fish,
and he took it and ate in their presence.

Luke 24: 36-42

THE WALK

It is easy to be discouraged when the sources of our
hope have been destroyed. We often collapse under the
weight of our hopelessness, when the boat seems to be
drowning. Getting the vision back, trying to resuscitate
our trust and our hopes and dreams, is hard to come to
terms with, when it has been taken away and stomped
on. Jesus provides an atypical kind of proof—his dam-
aged and mutilated body. He does not dazzle us with
the marks of death being erased. Rather, he shows us
his wounded hands and feet. Jesus becomes one with
us with our bruises and wounds. It is intentionally and
specifically, the marks of his suffering that provides for
all of us a true victory over the injustice of death. Restoration and reconciliation can only occur as a result
of our injuries. We have to face and reckon with the
wounds, injustices, and concrete evil that poisons our
world. That is the first step. We have to look at it, touch
and feel it, so we can heal it. We do so not to induce us
into revenge, or to awaken pity. We sit in the pain and
taste it, because there we see the incredible greatness
of God's saving activity in our lives. If we ignore these
bruises and wounds, then we are most assuredly seeing
ghosts, not the real presence of a healing God. When we
open our eyes and touch and see our brokenness, then
we can join Christ in eating that piece of broiled fish.

The Secret Room

THE SEVENTH STATION

Locked Room

THE WORD

When it was evening on that day,
the first day of the week,
and the doors of the house where the disciples had met
were locked for fear of the Jews,
Jesus came and stood among them and said,
"Peace be with you."
After he said this,
he showed them his hands and his side.
Then the disciples rejoiced when they saw the Lord.
Jesus said to them again,
"Peace be with you. As the Father has sent me, so I
send you."
When he had said this,
he breathed on them and said to them,
"Receive the Holy Spirit.
If you forgive the sins of any, they are forgiven them;
if you retain the sins of any, they are retained."

John 20:19-23

THE WALK

We fear death. It seems so final. Its pain grabs us by the throat and so we most certainly will want to lock the doors, to isolate, to hide. In these times, we yearn for security, but Jesus enters through our sealed hearts, offering peace. This greeting of peace, of *shalom*, is a peace of wholeness for all. What is broken is now restored. It is impossible for God's way and heart to be murdered or silenced. "Peace be with you" means that while death, pain, sadness and suffering will always be with us – it will not be the final word. It will not win. It will not be our destiny. Receiving and being filled with the Holy Spirit is once again, a commissioning. This commission is not to help design and structure an organization or movement, nor is it a guidebook for all of the administrative tasks and objectives that so often are consuming our attention. The commission is not to develop doctrines, creeds, or to judge. We are being taught, most simply yet directly, to forgive. We are in desperate need of forgiveness in ourselves, our world, in our relationships, and in our church. There is so much "non" shalom in our world: greed, torture, unrest, abuse, racism, lies, injustice and so much more. To show and offer forgiveness is to be given a second chance. That is the work of the Spirit. That is what is being asked of us all.

THE EIGHTH STATION

Thomas

THE WORD

A week later his disciples were again in the house,
and Thomas was with them.
Although the doors were shut,
Jesus came and stood among them and said,
"Peace be with you."
Then he said to Thomas,
"Put your finger here and see my hands.
Reach out your hand and put it in my side.
Do not doubt but believe."
Thomas answered him,
"My Lord and my God!"
Jesus said to him,
"Have you believed because you have seen me?
Blessed are those who have not seen
and yet have come to believe."

John 20:26-29

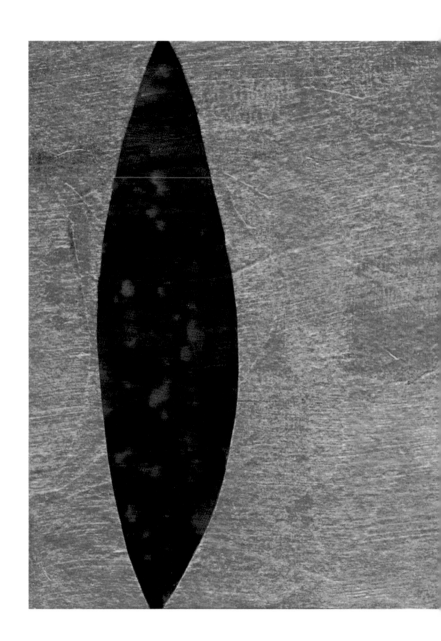

Into the Wound

THE WALK

Far too often, we need to be convinced. We want proof that we can see and touch, like Thomas. But here we find that the promise is more than real. It is the truth. Jesus truly has risen above the dagger of death. This is the final verdict, and it is anything but ambiguous. It is specific and filled with detail. Remember that earlier, in the Gospel of John, we are told that Thomas only agreed to die with Jesus. Resurrection was not part of what Thomas had signed on for (John 11:16). In these times, we follow the surrender of Thomas' cry, "My Lord and my God!" to be on our lips at all times, especially when we see the evidence of life spitting in the eye of death. We want evidence. That is OK. But our hearts yearn for more than that, they yearn for acceptance and assurance. We live our days, moving back and forth between skepticism and faith. So evidence is put before us. It cannot be argued. We can see it. We can believe it. Our surrendering to the Lordship of Jesus is an act of faith that renounces Ceasar or any other power as holding authority in our lives. And as a result, hope springs inwardly, outwardly, and eternally.

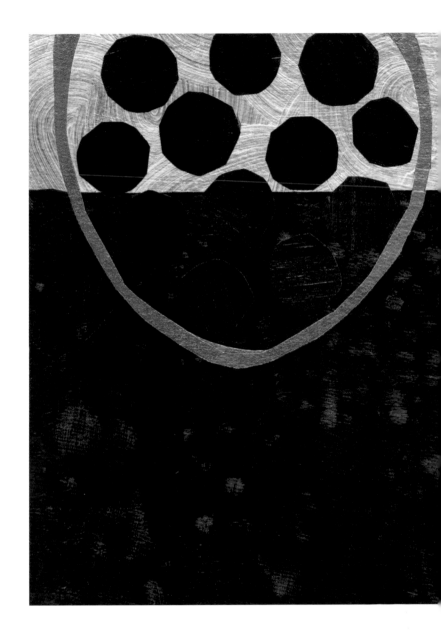

The Willing Catch

THE NINTH STATION

On the Shore

Just after daybreak, Jesus stood on the beach;
but the disciples did not know that it was Jesus.
Jesus said to them,
"Children, you have no fish, have you?"
They answered him, "No."
He said to them,
"Cast the net to the right side of the boat,
and you will find some."
So they cast it,
and now they were not able to haul it in
because there were so many fish.
That disciple whom Jesus loved said to Peter,
"It is the Lord!"
When Simon Peter heard that it was the Lord,
he put on some clothes, for he was naked,
and jumped into the sea.
But the other disciples came in the boat,
dragging the net full of fish,

for they were not far from the land,
only about a hundred yards off.
When they had gone ashore,
they saw a charcoal fire there, with fish on it,
and bread.

Jesus said to them,
"Come and have breakfast."
Now none of the disciples dared to ask him,
"Who are you?" because they knew it was the Lord.
Jesus came and took the bread and gave it to them,
and did the same with the fish.
This was now the third time
that Jesus appeared to the disciples
after he was raised from the dead.

John 21:4-9, 12-14

THE WALK

It is interesting to note that while the Gospels are filled
with stories of fishing, the followers of Jesus never catch
anything without his intervention. If we truly want to
share in the mission and ministry of serving others,
we need Christ by our side, guiding and feeding us.
He is always waiting, eager to feed and nourish us.
We need to remember that the Last Supper was really
not the last supper at all. Here, Jesus invites us all to
breakfast—which is a meal to begin the day. This is
the new beginning of eating and drinking with Jesus.
It always brings about something new, a new and fresh
start. These "table times" are when we are invited to be
close to the Lord, to truly find communion with God.
From this point forward, wherever we go, however we
are living, God dwells with us. When we take time to

avoid fast food, and really dine together, we have the blessed gift of being able to dwell and immerse ourselves in the most sacred aspects of relationship. Our need to always be on the go keeps us from "wasting time" with God. When we eat together, we pray together. When we pray together, regardless of outcomes, God is with us in the mix.

Love and Revelation

THE TENTH STATION

Peter

THE WORD

When they had finished breakfast,
Jesus said to Simon Peter,
"Simon son of John, do you love me more
than these?"
He said to him,
"Yes, Lord; you know that I love you."
Jesus said to him, "Feed my lambs."
A second time he said to him,
"Simon son of John, do you love me?"
He said to him,
"Yes, Lord; you know that I love you."
Jesus said to him, "Tend my sheep."
He said to him the third time,
"Simon son of John, do you love me?"
Peter felt hurt because he said to him the third time,
"Do you love me?"
And he said to him,
"Lord, you know everything;

you know that I love you."
Jesus said to him, "Feed my sheep.

John 21:15-17

THE WALK

There is, for all of us, times when our overactive or hyperactive selves take over. Many of us always have to be talking or moving or producing. Here we have an opportunity to find a way to survive and overcome the forces that often strangle our direction. We know all too well that Peter's three fold proclamation of love for Jesus, was preceded by and equally intense three-fold denial. But now, Peter's unfaithfulness is replaced and reoriented by knitting and embracing his total self to the heart of Christ. And in turn, Christ does not haunt Peter with his sin, but rather rejoices with him in this new reality of not only restoration, but also the call to serve lavishly and without hesitation. We so easily and too readily can find ourselves lost in darkness. These memories of our own spiritual hunger, of our failure to see the Body of Christ in the actual living and breathing members of the Body of Christ, will not be able to cover up or dilute the brightness of the light of Christ. For now, the Risen Christ has not ended his tireless cause of calling us, feeding us, and building us up in our relationships and in the world. If we truly love, our response then is to feed others – and in doing so, becoming a true sacramental presence, not through our words, but through the example of our lives.

THE ELEVENTH STATION

Mission

THE WORD

Jesus came and said to them,
"All authority in heaven and on earth has been given
to me.
Go therefore and make disciples of all nations,
baptizing them in the name of the Father
and of the Son and of the Holy Spirit,
and teaching them to obey everything
that I have commanded you.
And remember, I am with you always,
to the end of the age."

Matthew 28:18-20

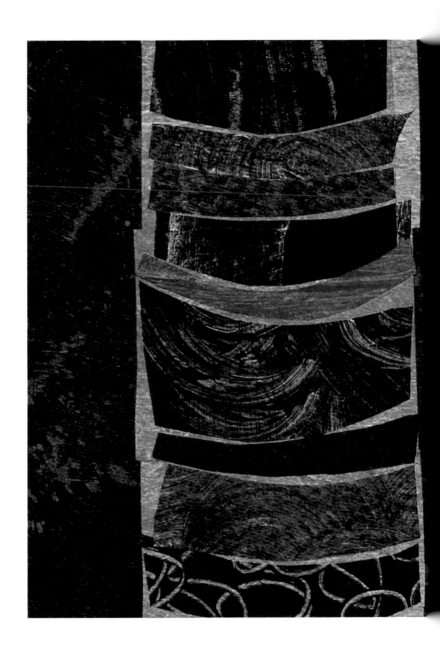

The Way of Water

THE WALK

What Christ is asking of us, is, honestly, an impossible task. It can throw us totally off guard and overwhelm us. How can we possibly answer such a call? Our response can only be to completely bow before the awesome strength and compassion of God. We can only accomplish the smallest aspects of God's reign, when we truly accept and act in a way that acknowledges that God is in charge of the destiny of the universe. We need to invest fully, and be willing to accept the direction of the Spirit. To be a disciple is to be a student. Good students are watching, practicing under the guidance of a teacher or mentor, learning from mistakes, and always "wiring in" our successes. To follow Christ is to be a life-long learner. We never graduate. This is the case not only for us as individuals, but also with the Church. We are a divided community, a fragile one filled with doubt, possessing only the tiniest particle of understanding this triune God of ours. With these things at the center, we are still being asked to plunge in totally, into the world with everything we have learned from God, realizing that without God we are nothing, and that with God, we can embrace an authority that can make disciples, first of ourselves, and then toward everyone we meet.

Ascension

THE TWELFTH STATION

Ascension

THE WORD

> As they were watching, he was lifted up,
> and a cloud took him out of their sight.
> While he was going
> and they were gazing up toward heaven,
> suddenly two men in white robes stood by them.
> They said,
> …"why do you stand looking up toward heaven?
> This Jesus who has been taken up from you
> into heaven,
> will come in the same way as you saw him go
> into heaven."

Acts: 1:11

THE WALK

Luke, who was the author of the Acts of the Apostles, and whose name means "bearer of the light," is revealing, or rather, "enlightening" us, that it is not only the human Jesus being taken up into the heart of God, but all of us. We live and move in times of great anxiety and insecurity. We experience abuse, violence, oppression and extreme poverty. We are confronted with the reality of suffering and death almost every day. In the midst of all of this, we are called, and we attempt with the best of intentions and with very passionate minds and hearts, to bring about healing and justice. We do not do it alone. We make this walk with Jesus, always united to God's compassionate heart. God came, and continues to, live in communion with us, to be home with us in our humanity. To restore the world, to rise up beyond it and enter into God's lavish care, means that we first need to become one with the world, to see it as *home*. And then we pray for this world—which includes all of us—to be taken up into the heart of God. So we dwell in our every day lives. And similarly, we ascend.

THE THIRTEENTH STATION

Mary and the Disciples

THE WORD

When they had entered the city,
they went to the room upstairs where they
were staying,
Peter, and John, and James, and Andrew,
Philip and Thomas, Bartholomew and Matthew,
James son of Alphaeus, and Simon the Zealot,
and Judas son of James.
All these were constantly devoting themselves
to prayer,
together with certain women,
including Mary the mother of Jesus,
as well as his brothers.

Acts 1:13-14

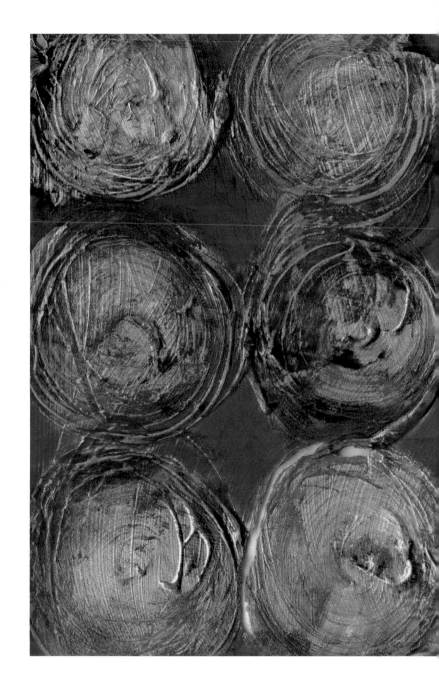

Remembering Is What We Do Together

THE WALK

Being constantly devoted to prayer is a great ideal, but no easy thing to accomplish. Yet at the same time, no great action can be accomplished with its absence. The work of God's reign, the ongoing resurrection so deeply needed, requires it to be inclusive. At this moment, we sow the seeds of such inclusion with the early church engaging in the life of prayer with "certain women." In the times of the early Church and ancient society, women were considered to be of lower status, so the fact that "Mary, the mother of Jesus" is at the center of this new life of prayer, is no small matter. This is an example for us to follow, to pray and work for the destruction of self-centeredness, so that the greater mission of God's path is accomplished in new and untested ways. Being a close-knit community is one thing. But to cling to an exclusive group of like-minded people is not living according to the heart of God. Our life of prayer, and its leadership is to be shared among a grand diversity of cultures, gender-blind, and not concerned with being perfect or a perception of necessary worthiness. Resurrection means rising above old patterns that lock people out. True prayer is prayer rooted in the fact that God speaks to everyone, everywhere. Now, that is resurrection.

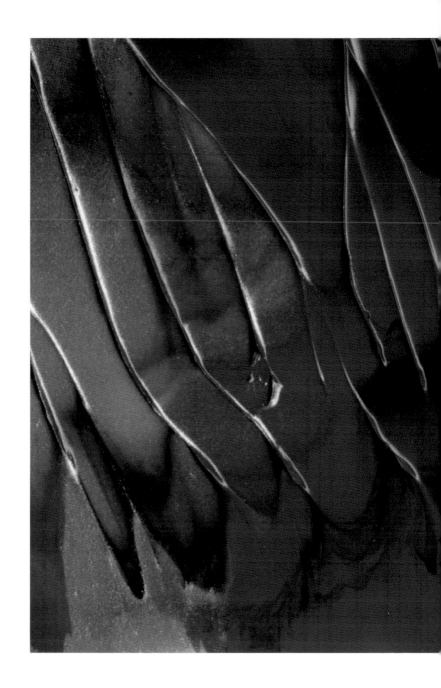

Pentecost Fire

THE FOURTEENTH STATION

Pentecost

THE WORD

When the day of Pentecost had come,
They were all together in one place.
And suddenly from heaven there came a sound
like the rush of a violent wind,
and it filled the entire house where they were sitting.

Divided tongues, as of fire,
appeared among them,
and a tongue rested on each of them.
All of them were filled with the Holy Spirit
and began to speak in other languages,
as the Spirit gave them ability.

Acts 2:1-4

THE WALK

The work of the Spirit is always more powerful, more authentic, and more clearly directed when we come together. Not by going through the motions of a false sense of unity, but rather, as an intentional commitment to inclusion, which is often messy, but always interesting. Resurrection is not a clean enterprise, as it twists and turns differently for different people. For Jesus it was one way, and ever since his rising, the many interpretations and activities of the Spirit of God have travelled and been made known in so many varied ways. The tongues of fire are the source of a diverse rainbow of power, a power not taken, but *received* in not only many unique languages but through the many different and glorious ways in which we receive and respond to the gifts of the breath of God. This power purifies, enlightens, reignites, and blasts us out of our complacency in order that we might act. We, the Church, the Body of Christ, desperately need the Holy Spirit to bring about and amplify the dreams, signs and wonders that came not only on that marvelous day of Pentecost, but to continue blowing within and among every moment of every day. To the extent that we are open to receive it, the Spirit of God is here, ready to fill us. The call is to do more than merely receive it, as something to hoard. The question is, will we also release it?

THE FIFTEENTH STATION

Paul

THE WORD

Meanwhile Saul,
still breathing threats and murder
against the disciples of the Lord,
went to the high priest and asked him
for letters to the synagogues at Damascus,
so that if he found any who belonged to the Way,
men or women,
he might bring them bound to Jerusalem.
Now as he was going along
and approaching Damascus,
suddenly a light from heaven flashed around him.
He fell to the ground and heard a voice saying to him,
"Saul, Saul, why do you persecute me?"
He asked, "Who are you, Lord?"
The reply came,
"I am Jesus, whom you are persecuting.
But get up and enter the city,
and you will be told what you are to do."

Acts 9:1-6

Finding the Focus

THE WALK

This is more than a story of one man's turning away from persecution and religious terrorism toward the early Christian community. This points to a more covert and overt insidious choice to victimize, deny and persecute the Christ who surrounds us in our world. Paul's complicity with such terrorizing of others is confronted, and speaks to all who claim God as their center, if we are to take our mission and discipleship seriously. The way of the resurrection must be a daily choice for all of us. This means we must confront the authenticity of our lives beyond our words and good wishes. Resurrection means ongoing renewal to stand in solidarity with all who are victimized and persecuted for who they are, what they believe, who they choose to love, how they choose to follow or not follow a particular path. Over and over again, we persecute far too many manifestations of "God among us." This story points to the need not to have a single dramatic conversion, but a daily practice and openness to being born again and again and again and again! This means to throw ourselves more deeply into the same margins that so many of our sisters and brothers find themselves. True conversion is doing more than picking up the pieces after our mistakes and vowing to never commit them again. Conversion is about taking the risk and taking up the cross, and working tirelessly toward rolling stones away so more tombs can be emptied.

NOTES

1. From *Be Born In Us Today*, Text and Music by David Haas. Copyright © 2001, GIA Publications, Inc. 7404 South Mason Avenue, Chicago, IL 60638. Used with permission. All rights reserved.

2. From *Look to Christ* by David Haas. Copyright © 2007, GIA Publications, Inc. 7404 South Mason Avenue, Chicago, IL 60638. Used with permission. All rights reserved.

3. From *Now We Remain* by David Haas. Copyright © 1983, GIA Publications, Inc. 7404 South Mason Avenue, Chicago, IL 60638. Used with permission. All rights reserved.

4. From *The Tomb Is Empty* by David Haas. Copyright © 2003, GIA Publications, Inc. 7404 South Mason Avenue, Chicago, IL 60638. Used with permission. All rights reserved.

All of the musical examples listed above are available as a downloadble MP3 music files, available from GIA Publications. www.giamusic.com

ABOUT THE AUTHOR

David Haas is from Eagan, Minnesota where he is the director of The Emmaus Center for Music, Prayer and Ministry, in addition to serving as Animator for the Taizé Prayer Community at Cretin-Derham Hall in St. Paul, Minnesota. Highly regarded as one of the pre-eminent composers of liturgical music in the English-speaking world, he has produced and published over 50 collections and recordings with GIA Publications, and his music has been translated into many languages and appears in hymnals of various Christian denominations throughout the world. In 1991 David was nominated for a Grammy Award for the recording of *I Shall See God* and is the founder and executive director for *Music Ministry Alive!*, (www.musicministryalive.com) an international liturgical music formation institute for high school and college age youth. He has travelled extensively as a workshop presenter and concert performer in all 50 states, as well as Canada, Australia, The Bahamas, England, Ireland, Germany, Italy, Israel, Greece and Turkey. He has authored over 25 books in the areas of liturgy, religious education, youth ministry and spirituality, including *Welcome, Faithful Presence: A Week of Praying the Hours with Henri Nouwen*, and in May 2015 he received an Honorary Doctorate in Humane Letters from the University of Portland in Oregon.

ABOUT THE ARTIST

Jan Richardson is an artist, writer, and ordained minister in the United Methodist Church. Known for such popular books as *Night Visions* and *In Wisdom's Path*, she serves as director of The Wellspring Studio, LLC, and makes her home in Florida. www.janrichardson.com